The Little Airline that Could!

Eastern Provincial Airways
The First Fifteen Years

Marsh Jones

The Little Airline that Could!

Eastern Provincial Airways
The First Fifteen Years

Marsh Jones

Creative Publishers
St. John's, Newfoundland
1998

© 1998, Marshall B. Jones

The Canada Council FOR THE ARTS SINCE 1957	Le Conseil des Arts du Canada DEPUIS 1957

We acknowledge the support of the Canada Council for the Arts for our publishing program.

The publisher acknowledges the support of the Department of Tourism, Culture and Recreation, Government of Newfoundland and Labrador, towards the publication of this book.

All rights reserved. No part of this work covered by the copyrights hereon may be reproduced or used in any form or by any means—graphic, electronic or mechanical—without the prior written permission of the publisher. Any requests for photocopying, recording, taping or information storage and retrieval systems of any part of this book shall be directed in writing to the Canadian Reprography Collective, 214 King Street West, Suite 312, Toronto, Ontario M5H 2S6.

Cover — David Peckford

∝ Printed on acid-free paper

Published by
CREATIVE BOOK PUBLISHING
a division of 10366 Newfoundland Limited
a Robinson-Blackmore Printing & Publishing associated company
P.O. Box 8660, St. John's, Newfoundland A1B 3T7

Printed in Canada by:
ROBINSON-BLACKMORE PRINTING & PUBLISHING

Canadian Cataloguing in Publication Data

Jones, Marsh 1926–

    The little airline that could!

    ISBN 1-895387-95-7

1. Eastern Provincial Airways (1963) Limited.
2. Aeronautics, Commercial — Newfoundland — History.
3. Air pilots — Canada — Biography. I. Title.

HE9815.E37J6 1998   387.7'09718   C98-950151-5

DEDICATION
This book is dedicated to my granddaughters
Shelly, Julie and Lauren
and grandsons
Richard, Marshall and Stirling

LIST OF PHOTOGRAPHS

Piper Cub VO-ABD	3
Marsh Jones in Original Epa Uniform	9
Cessna T-50 VO-ACE	10
Seebee CF-DKQ	11
Stinson StationWagon CF-GPH	26
Stonson Station Wagon CF-GPH on floats	27
Norseman CF-GMP	31
Norseman, Beaver, Norseman at Millertown Junction	32
Norseman at Pudups Lake	36
Beaver CF-FHS	38
Norseman CF-GPM at Torbay Airport	44
Norseman CF-GPM departing Shediac, N.B.	48
Avro Anson at Millertown Junction	49
Anson CF-GSA through the ice at Millertown Junction	51
Beaver and Norseman at Quidi Vidi	53
W.H. (Bill) Harris	54
Marsh Jones and Norseman CF-GPI	58
Inflight photo of Beaver CF-GBD	60
Marsh Jones at Grand Falls, Labrador	62
Beaver on Wheel/Skis	67
Beaver CF-GBF at crash site	76
A.J. Lewingtom/Roy Cooper	79
Beaver aircraft on Gander Lake	80
Piper Cub CF-GPD	81
Canso CF-HFL	83
De Havilland Otter	84
Norseman CF-GPM through the ice at St. Anthony	86
Salvage operations, Otter CF-GCV at Black Tickle	87
Delivery of Fleet Canuck to Fundy Flying Club	88
Fleet Canuck CF-DEN	89
Lockheed CF-BXE	90
Beaver CF-IHK wrecked at St. Anthony	91
Helicopter CF-IVE	92
Seebee CF-DLS	93
Canso CF-HFL crashed 75 miles northeast of Goose Bay	102
Captain Ben Rivard/Co-pilot Ron Smith	103
Canso being airlifted and on ramp at Goose Airport	104
Royal Gull CF-ILU	105
DC-3 CF-JNR	108
Canso CF-CRP at Ivigtut, Greenalnd	109
Otter CF-LEA at Fort Chimo	111
Otter CF-LEA and Beaver CF-GQU at Resolution	113
Canso C-CRP refuelling Otter CF-LEA at Fort Chimo	122
Otters on the ramp at Godthab, Greenland	123
Otter CF-MIT on arrival at Gander from Toronto	125
Leaving Hanger 20 for Hanger 22, Gander	125
DC-3s CF-QBM and CF-CEW on ramp at Gander	127
c-46s Cf-NAD and CF-NAE	128
Otters at northern Greenland	132/133
Canso CF-CRP, Godthab, Greenland	133
Chesley A. Crosbie	139
Handley Page Dart Herald	142
Hawker Siddley 748	142
British Air Traders Cavair	143
Boeing 737	143

CONTENTS

Foreword		ix
Acknowledgements		xi
Map of Newfoundland		xii
Map of Labrador		xiii
Map of Newfoundland, Labrador and Greenland		xiv
Chapter 1	Pre-Eastern Provincial Airlines	1
Chapter 2	Employed by EPA	9
Chapter 3	Early Flights: Seabee and Stinson	11
Chapter 4	The Airmail Service	31
Chapter 5	Early Flights: Norseman and Beaver	37
Chapter 6	Flight Operations: 1951	49
Chapter 7	Flight Operations: 1952	55
Chapter 8	Flight Operations: 1953	67
Chapter 9	Flight Operations: 1954	75
Chapter 10	Flight Operations: 1955	83
Chapter 11	Flight Operations: 1956	91
Chapter 12	Flight Operations: 1957	101
Chapter 13	Flight Operations: 1958	109
Chapter 14	Flight Operations: 1959	117
Chapter 15	Flight Operations: 1960	121
Chapter 16	Bushline to Airline: 1961	127
Chapter 17	Flight Operations: 1962	135
Chapter 18	We Lose our President	139
Chapter 19	Purchase of Handley Page Dart Heralds	141
Chapter 20	1964: Eastern Provincial Airlines (1963) Ltd.	147
Chapter 21	Conclusion	149
Appendices		151

Foreword
Harry R. Steele

*A*t the time I joined Eastern Provincial Airways' Board of Directors in 1972, the airline had been in operation for twenty-three years. It was started on a shoestring budget, with a couple of small airplanes and hopes for a bright future by Newfoundland businessman Ches Crosbie and his managing director and pilot, Eric Blackwood. Marsh Jones was its first full-time pilot.

Those were the days of seat-of-the-pants flying with little more than a map, compass and radio to enable pilots of the fledgling airline to carry out their assigned duties. Flying conditions were often harsh and unforgiving; landing sites were largely untested, and much was left to the pilot's judgement and initiative. But the little airline survived, and grew.

Marsh Jones — who served with the airline in a variety of positions from 1949 until his retirement in June, 1979 as Vice President of Operations responsible for all flying — was one of those hardworking intuitive people whose efforts brought EPA from the status of a bushline to that of a scheduled airline.

The story, as it unfolds in this book, is of course from Marsh Jones' viewpoint. There were many people who helped shape the airline, from its directors, administrators and pilots to its engineers, mechanics and other support personnel. These were the people who *were* Eastern Provincial Airlines, and Marsh worked closely with them all.

Marsh Jones' narrative ends in 1964 with the purchase of Maritime Central Airways. That was the era of the most significant growth. The airline would continue to grow and eventually become part of Canadian Airlines, but it was the early years which formed the basis for the company which it eventually became, and it was Marsh Jones and people like him whose efforts made the airline such a unique success.

Acknowledgements

*S*o many of my friends have encouraged me to write the story of EPA that to name them would be a fearful task. Fearful in that I might forget someone. I wish however to acknowledge the encouragement I've received from Dr. Gus Rowe in his constructive critique during the writing of the manuscript and my daughter Lesley for for her help in typing and some of the initial editing. Also, a special thanks to Captain Ben Rivard who so kindly contributed his computer equipment and talent in the typing and editing of this book.

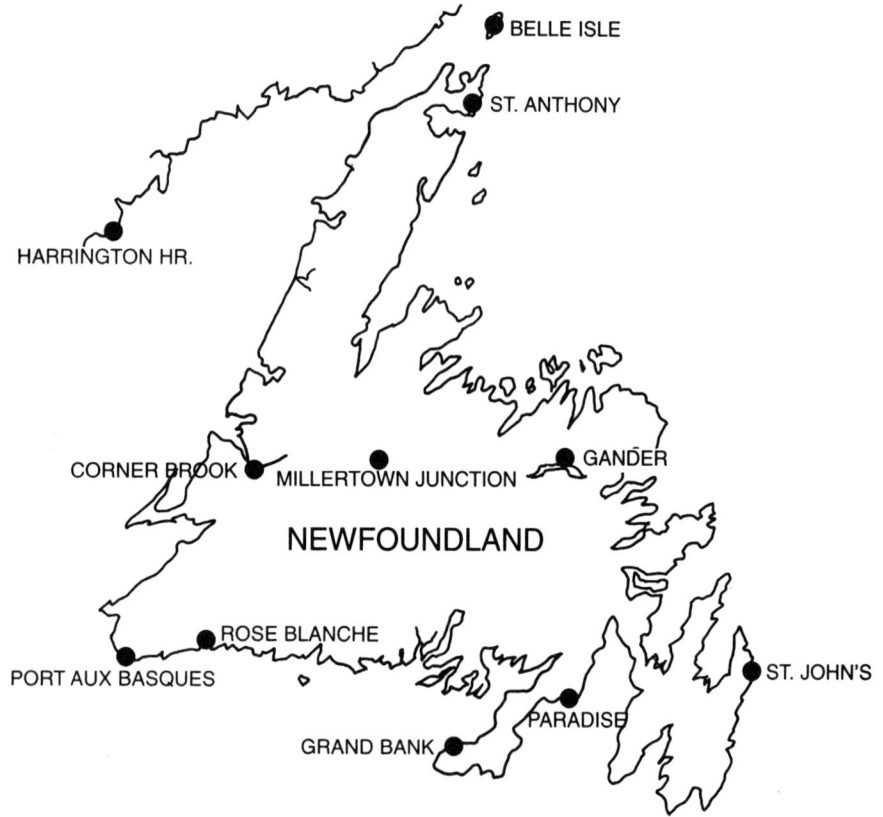

Not drawn to scale

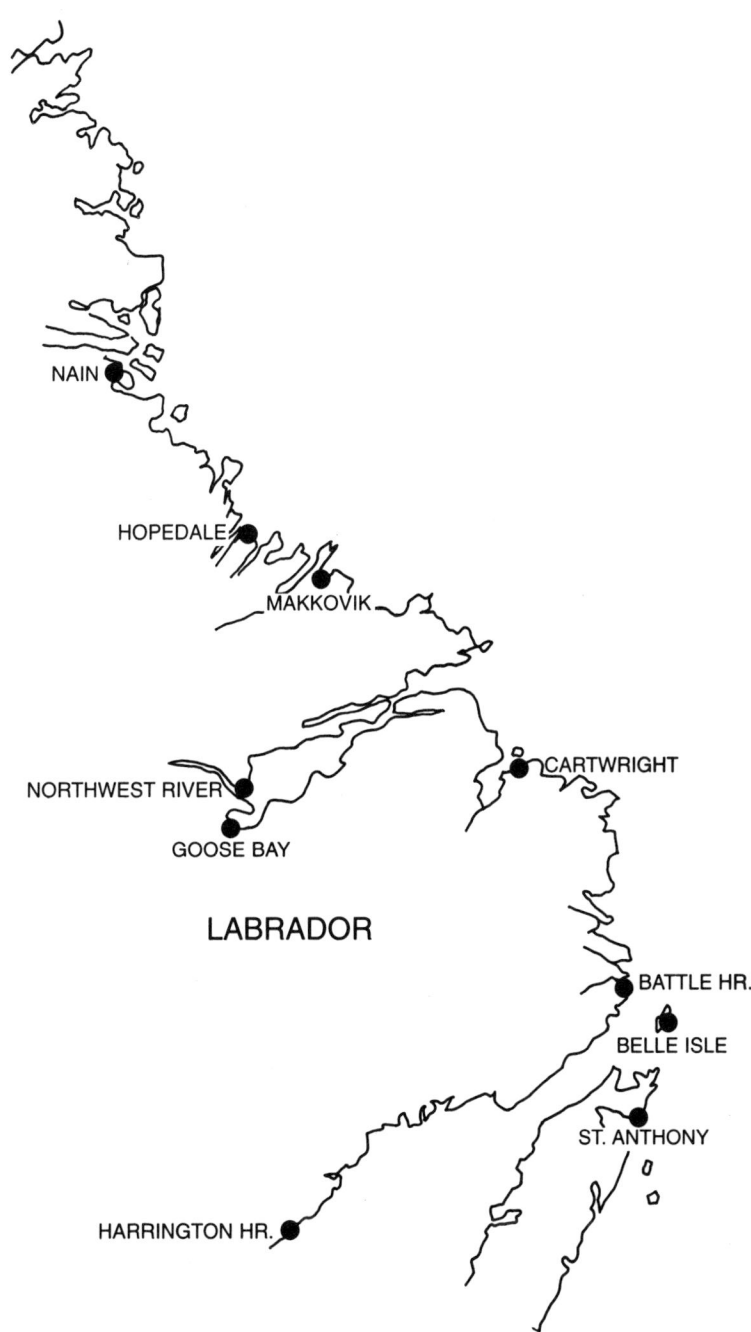

Not drawn to scale

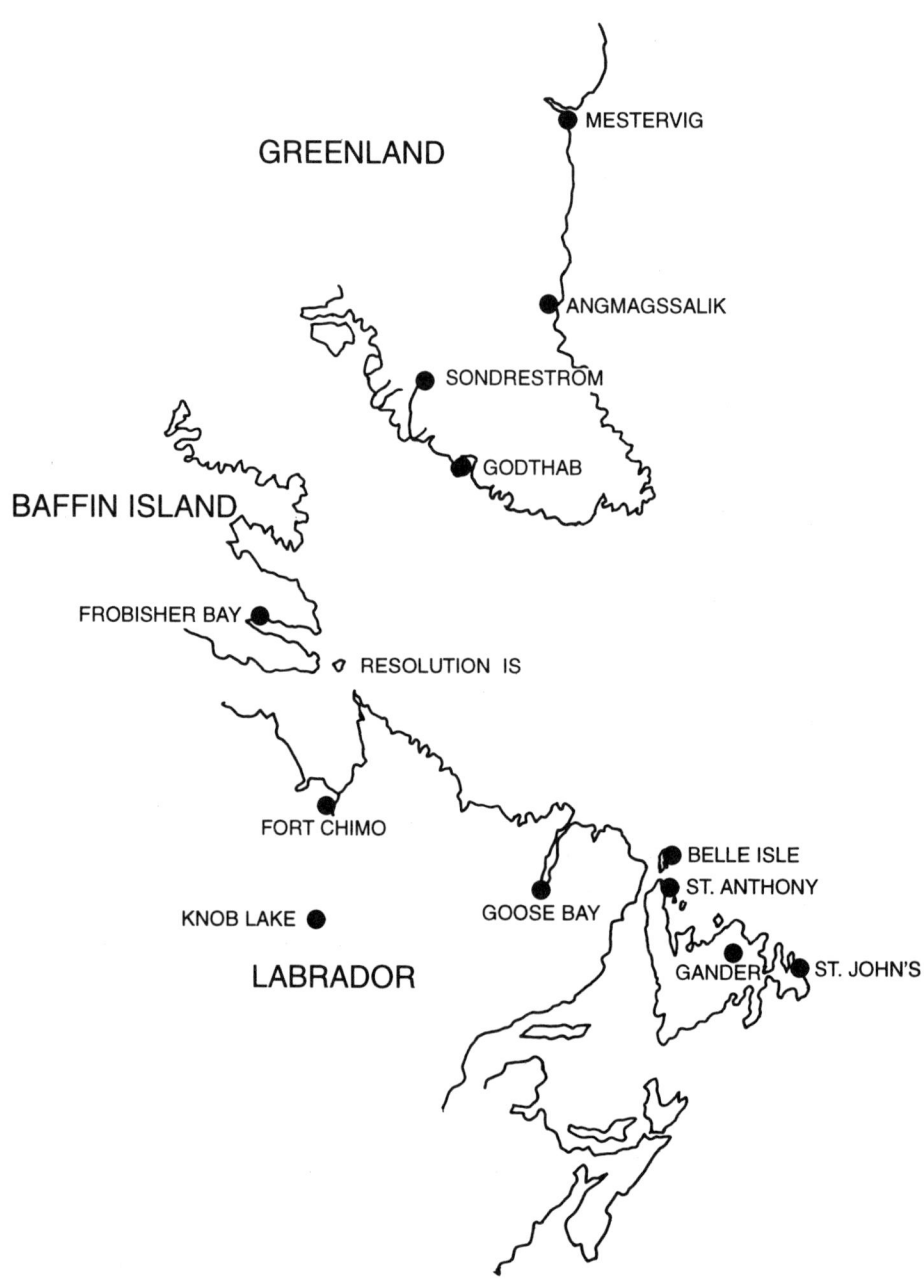

Not drawn to scale

Chapter 1

Pre-EPA

My career in aviation covered many phases of aircraft operations but the period of which I have the fondest memories and nostalgia are the early years. They were probably the hardest years and certainly the least remunerative ones. My average earnings per month for my first year with EPA was $300.00 and even then there were periods when it was necessary to wait for your pay as there was no money available. But I was very young and my love for airplanes and the sense of adventure tended to offset that.

I started flight training in the RCAF at #2 SFTS Uplands near Ottawa and trained on Harvard MK II aircraft, receiving my wings on January 19, 1945, just prior to my nineteenth birthday.

After graduation, and because things were winding down in Europe with no further pilot requirements, we were honourably released from the RCAF. At a loss for what to do I obtained work as a construction worker on the new Sunnybrook Hospital in Toronto. Later on in June I had a brief stint in the Royal Navy Fleet Air Arm in England hoping to get out to the Pacific Theatre. This however didn't amount to anything as the war in the pacific was over in August, and I found myself back in Newfoundland at the end of November wondering what to do.

As there was nothing in flying available I decided to go to sea as my father had before me. However, late in 1946 when off on holidays, I met my wife Enid and decided to stay ashore. I had also heard that a flying company, NASSCO, was being formed by Eric Blackwood. I jumped at the chance of anything relating to my first love: flying. However, it was not to be, as commitment had been made to other pilots.

This did not discourage me as I knew sooner or later I'd be lucky.

So I went to a vocational school and graduated as a refrigeration mechanic and obtained a job with Beverage Sales Ltd., a soft drink bottling company.

Late in 1947 Hedley Tuff and I bought a Piper Cub wreck from NASSCO. This airplane had crashed on take-off in Blanc Sablon, Labrador on March 19, 1946 and was a write-off. We bought it for $25.00, and a time-expired Continental Engine for $150.00. Over the next two months we repaired it to our satisfaction and in mid-December 1947 flew it off the snow covered ice at Long Pond just north of St. John's.

It had one instrument in the panel — An oil pressure gauge. The windshield was not perspex but heavy celuloid and bent back when in flight; there were no side windows, no engine cowl and no exhaust muffler — just straight pipes out of each of the four cylinders. We were very proud of it and flew a number of people on flights over St. John's. One notable passenger John Murphy who was later to become Mayor of St. John's.

It wasn't very long before we received a summons to appear before court. We were charged on three counts:
- I didn't have a pilot licence;
- The aircraft was repaired by unlicensed persons and using unapproved methods of repair;
- The aircraft was not registered in Newfoundland.

Of course we pleaded guilty and had to sign a $100 bond that we would not fly the aircraft again.

We then bought an airworthy Piper Cub from NASSCO for $1000.00. I qualified for my private pilot's licence (#8)

Piper Cub VO-ABD
Avalon Flying Service

and shortly thereafter received commercial pilot's licence #14.

We operated the aircraft under the name Avalon Flying Service. I was still working with Beverage Sales and did the flying in my spare time. We were mainly engaged in passenger sightseeing flights from Torbay airport to Bell Island, charging $3.00 for a fifteen minute flight. We also did flights spotting schools of mackerel fish for a local fish company. Our biggest job was with the Responsible Government League in 1948, prior to the referendum to decide whether or not Newfoundland would join Canada. Geoff Stirling, on behalf of the Responsible Government League, supplied a loudspeaker and transmitter which Tuffy and I installed in the Cub. We would fly over the various settlements at 500 feet and Don Jamieson, who was a well-known broadcaster, would transmit the political propaganda. Along with Responsible Government they were also advocating economic union with the United States.

After covering the area within 100 miles of St. John's, the Cub was changed from wheels to floats and with Paul

Johnson as my loudspeaker operator, I covered the area of White Bay, Notre Dame Bay and Bonavista Bay.

We crashed taking off from Deadman's pond in Gander on our way back to St. John's.

The aircraft was grossly overloaded, particularly for the take-off run available. I managed to get airborne but with very little rate of climb I knew I could not clear the trees on the shore line. Therefore I purposely stuck a wing in the water and pranged.[1] The floats were demolished and the left wing tip was damaged. Tuffy flew out to Gander the next day on TCA with the wheel gear, and the following day we repaired the damage and flew her back to St. John's.

During this time I had been giving Tuffy flying instruction. In August of 1948 he was ready for his first solo cross-country flight. The flight was to be from St. John's to Gander via the headlands of Conception and Trinity Bays. This was necessary because in a single-engine aircraft on wheels, where it is illegal to fly over water you must stay within gliding distance of land. Anyway Tuffy made it to Gander refuelled and started back for St. John's.

Approaching the area of Sunnyside in Trinity Bay the weather started to deteriorate with low stratus clouds speeding in from Placentia Bay, to the point where he could not continue. So he turned east and flew up the north coast of Trinity Bay hoping he might spot a clearing across to the south shore. By this time the whole area was closing in and as he was running low on fuel he realized he would have to land somewhere. He was flying below the hills over the water and with no level area in sight he was becoming a little worried. He had passed a small settlement so he decided to return to it and make a forced landing, in the water if necessary. On

---

1 A word for crash, common among airmen, particularly those who flew with the RAF and RCAF in WWII.

approaching the settlement from the sea he saw a small clearing with a fenced in potato patch on one corner and a little graveyard on the opposite corner. By now he was desperate. He made a powered approach at 40 mph and plunked the cub down in between the potato patch and the graveyard. The picket fence caught the right lift strut which caused her to stop and swing with no damage except for 2" off one tip of the propeller. Tuffy was not even shaken up!

Looking around he realized he would never be able to take off so decided he would have to dismantle the plane and take it by boat to some place where he could take off. At the time there were no roads on this part of the coast.

He borrowed some tools from a local fisherman who said he could take the airplane up the bay on his boat the next morning, where the aircraft could be loaded on a truck for St. John's. The wings were taken off and the following morning the aircraft was lowered down a vertical cliff about twenty feet to the deck of the schooner. About three hours later they arrived at the head of Trinity Bay, near Cavendish, where a truck was hired. Tuffy and the aircraft arrived at Torbay airport late in the afternoon, none the worse for wear. I hadn't even known he had gone to Gander on his cross-country flight, and fortunately he had phoned the Gander Control Tower of his forced landing shortly after it happened. He did not however get credit for his cross-country flight, and he was required to do another one.

Tuffy eventually went on to become a pilot with Trans Canada Airline, later Air Canada, retired in 1985 as a senior captain on Boeing 747. He lived near me in Nova Scotia and had a small Cesna 170 floatplane which I enjoyed flying from time to time until he passed away in November 1993. He was sixty-six.

Avalon Flying Service 1948/49

Our particular aircraft, registered VO-ABD, was actually a Piper L4, an ex-army aircraft built for close air/ground support. It was a two-seat in tandem high wing monoplane, powered by a Continental 65 hp engine. It had a gross weight of 1220 lbs and a cruising speed of 73 mph. It was adaptable to wheel or float landing gear. After Confederation in 1949, the registration was changed to Canadian registration CF-GPD. The aircraft was operated by Avalon Flying Service from May 12, 1948 until it was sold to Eastern Provincial Airways Ltd. in October, 1949.

This little aircraft was my first introduction to commercial flying. I had just obtained my commercial pilot licence, and Tuffy and I were anxious to make some money. Our first venture was sightseeing. We advertised "see your city from the air" $3.00 for a fifteen minute flight. We operated each evening and weekend from Hangar 2 at Torbay airport. The response was encouraging with Tuffy handling the ground operation and money, and me doing the flying!

We soon broadened our operation to include Bell Island. We would advertise ahead, then land at a field on Neary's farm. You could see the crowds of people on the field from miles away, making it necessary to make several passes overhead so they would clear a path for us to land. Eventually the runway at Bell Island was built on the same site.

One evening with nothing doing I decided to do a few aerobatics so I took off in the Cub and climbed eastward to 2000 feet over the coastal village of Torbay. I was doing a wing over stalled turn when the engine stopped. My immediate action was to lower the nose sharply hoping to windmill the propeller and get the engine started, as there was no internal starting system. I was about a mile out over the water from Torbay, and losing altitude fast with the prop showing no sign of turning and with the nose pointing straight down. When the altimeter passed through 1000 feet I realized I'd better start gliding and try and land in a field. The field I chose to land in had several cows grazing and a wooden longer² fence running through it. Well, I touched down on the first half of the field narrowly missing the cows, then through the longer fence knocking the longers flying and finally stopped nose down in a ditch in the second half of the field.

I surveyed the damage which consisted of a slightly bent left strut and a dent underneath the engine cowl. Luckily the propeller was not damaged. There were a few drops of water dropping from the carburettor intake and it finally hit me! "Carburettor icing." I had forgotten to pull on carburettor heat before throttling back on the wing over stalled turn. That is why the engine stopped!

I restarted the engine with no difficulty, took off and returned to Torbay airport with no one the wiser at the time except ME!

I had a call from Colin Storey one evening wanting to know if he could charter our aircraft to do some mackerel fish spotting. I arranged for him to meet me at Torbay airport the following morning and we were airborne bright and early. We flew across Trinity Bay to overhead Carbonear. Then on to Holyrood, Ferryland and back up the coast to Torbay. Colin was very pleased with the flight and arranged for another flight on September 28, at which time we spotted large schools of mackerel off the Harbour Grace area. Colin was very excited and wanted to know if I could land on the airstrip at Harbour Grace so he could phone his people to advise of the mackerel.

The airstrip had been used during pre-war days as a stopping point for trans-Atlantic attempts, but had been

---

2 Longers are small tree trunks, trimmed and used to make a rail fence,

closed effectively during the war by the army rolling large boulders onto the airstrip. We did land however, dodging the boulders with little difficulty as the Cub required very little landing distance. This flight was followed by another successful one on October 1, at which time another landing was made at Harbour Grace.

After I was employed by Eastern Provincial Airways in July 1949 I flew the aircraft quite often in flight instructing, and several times up until 1955 carrying winter mail to Notre Dame Bay points when we were desperate for aircraft. We could actually get 300 lbs of mail in the back seat area.

The aircraft was sold to Frank LeDrew of Corner Brook in July 1954.

Chapter 2

Employed by EPA

In early June 1949 Eric Blackwood, the Managing Director and only pilot with the newly formed Eastern Provincial Airways, advised me that if I would obtain an instructor rating and twin engine endorsement he would give me a job flying. Naturally I responded to this and on June 23 started training at the Moncton Flying Club.

I received my instructor and twin-engine ratings on July 9 and was hired by EPA on July 13, 1949, on which day I made my first flight in a Cessna Crane between St. John's and Gander.

This small twin-engine aircraft was used during World War II as a twin-engine trainer. It was powered by two 225 hp Jacobs L4MB radial engines. It could carry four passengers plus the pilot. EPA's first Cessna Crane was VO-ACE, which was badly damaged on its first ski equipped landing at La Scie in January 1945.

An effort was made in January 1950 to repair VO-ACE with replacement undercarriage and propellers. However the aircraft, flown by Hank Hicks, crashed after take-off ending its days on a wooded hillside at Stakes Pond near La Scie, White Bay.

Marsh Jones wearing original EPA uniform 1949

Cessna T-50 VO-ACE
Eric Blackwood, Jack Phennel, Emerson Blackwood
EPA's first aircraft
Quidi Vidi Lake, St. John's — 1949

A Cessna Crane, CF-FDR, had been purchased, mainly for its propellers and undercarriage, which would be used to repair VO-ACE in La Scie. However this aircraft was in excellent condition so another Cessna was purchased from Leavens Brothers in Toronto and it was this aircraft which was used for parts for VO-ACE.

It was with CF-FDR that EPA started its first unit toll passenger service between St. John's, Gander and Buchans. This service was continued through the summer of 1949 with very little success due to lack of public response and poor facilities. It was terminated in November 1949.

Chapter 3

Early Flights

SEABEE

The Republic RC-3 Seabee, a four-place single-engine amphibian first flew in November of 1944 and entered production in early 1946. It was revolutionary at the time and sold for $5000. It had many features: all-metal construction, a reversing propeller and a steerable, full-castering, side retracting tail wheel. Its four-place cabin with large side doors, right-hand windshield door and panoramic

Seabee CF-DKQ
on skis in Cartwright
1952

windows gave a 220 degree vision forward of the wing. Its 215 hp Franklyn six-cylinder engine was mounted on top of the single high wing. Unfortunately, the engine proved a little underpowered for its 3050 lbs gross take-off weight. It was nevertheless a very popular and versatile aircraft.

I made a number of flights with this aircraft during the summer of 1949, some of which I remember very clearly.

"HIGH AND DRY IN LABRADOR"
AUGUST 18 – 22, 1949.

The purpose of this flight was to take a 'Mr. Muir' — of Muir's Marble Works — and his daughter from Torbay (St. John's) to Baie Verte in White Bay, and from there to pick up a plumber, Ted Patey, at St. Anthony and fly him to the Cottage Hospital in Harrington Harbour on the north shore of Quebec Labrador, stay with him, and return him to St. Anthony when he'd finished his work. Don Patey, a new pilot with EPA, was to go along as an observer and to familiarize himself with the operation.

Don met me at the airport at 0730. We had the Seabee refuelled and checked the weather while we waited for our passengers to show up. The weather looked excellent for the next few days, with the exception of the Labrador Coast which could be marginal. Mr. Muir and his daughter arrived at 0800. After their baggage was loaded we started, taxied to runway 26, and after a long take-off run we were airborne and flying low over Windsor Lake. I had a preference for this particular runway with the Seabee, as Windsor Lake was off the western end and should something go wrong after take-off you could always land on the water. With a full tank of fuel (60 gallons), four fairly large people, and baggage, we were slightly over our maximum take-off weight and the Seabee was reluctant to climb.

Our flight path direct to Gander took us over Western Bay in Conception Bay, Hants Harbour, Irelands Eye in

Trinity Bay, then over Musgravetown and into Gander airport where we refuelled, and, after coffee, took off for Baie Verte. Visibility was excellent, and with light westerly winds we made a smooth water landing in Baie Verte and taxied up to an anchored open boat into which our passengers deplaned. (There were no seaplane facilities available there at that time.) We were airborne again in five minutes, climbing out smartly to the north and St. Anthony. What a difference two passengers and baggage could make to a Seabee's performance.

Our flight path took us from Baie Verte over Partridge Point, across White Bay to Conche, and direct to St. Anthony, where we landed after a flying time of one hour. We taxied to Don Pomeroy's wharf and tied up to the rear quarter of a boat docked there, and arranged for a drum of fuel to be lowered into the boat, from which we refuelled. Don Pomeroy was EPA's agent and stored a supply of aviation gas and a refuelling hand pump and strainer on the premises. With refuelling completed, I checked the oil level in the engine and topped up the tank. I noticed, as usual, that the tail section had a film of oil over it, which was normal as the O-ring seal in the actuating cylinder of the Hartzell propeller allowed some leaking during operation. It was for observation of the tail section in flight that a mirror was installed on the left lift strut below the wing, allowing the pilot to determine by the shade of oil on the tail how much oil remained in the tank.

After lunch at Don Patey's home, we picked up Ted Patey — the IGA[1] plumber — and his tools, and went to the aircraft which we'd left lying clear of the dock on a mooring line. Take-off at St, Anthony was routine, as we were well within

---

1 The International Grenfell Association provided medical services in Northern Newfoundland and Labrador.

weight limits due to less than full fuel and three persons on board.

Our flight was to take us over Flower's Cove and direct over the water to Harrington Harbour; however, on approaching the Strait of Belle Isle it was evident, as the cloud lowered, that we were running out of sky. We passed over Flower's Cove heading west over the water, which was looking very grey with wisps of low fog drifting in ever-increasing blankets.

It was time to retreat, and with a slow 180 degree turn we headed for Flower's Cove where we could be accommodated at the IGA nursing station. We landed in the harbour where, as a result of a slight swell, we skipped a few times and then settled on as the speed decreased. We taxied in and picked up a boat mooring, securing the aircraft with its own mooring bridle. A local man, Stephen Whalen, came out and took us to shore in his boat, after which we walked the short distance to the nursing station.

The weather forecast on the Doyle News Bulletin[2] that evening advised of good weather In Newfoundland, but possible fog on the north shore and the strait. The next morning dawned grey with about three mile's visibility. I decided to try as I could always land if the weather got too bad. The flight mileage was about 150, or one and one-half hour's flying time.

After breakfast, we arranged for a boat to take us out to the Seabee which was riding at anchor in the harbour. We carried out our aircraft check, pumped out a little water from the compartments, started up, and after a warm-up, took off

---

2 The Doyle News Bulletin, sponsored by Gerald S. Doyle Limited, was heard nightly on CBC (and its predecessor VONF) and was a source for the sharing of information to areas where communication was difficult and expensive.

out the harbour into a light southwest wind. At 300 feet we were into the overcast, so I dropped down a little until we were clear of cloud and headed towards Blanc Sablon, having decided to make landfall there and proceed down the coast, keeping just off the numerous headlands.

Every thing went well until just north of Harrington Harbour, in Aylmer Sound. The overcast became fog which I could not get under. I circled several times, hoping for a break, but finally decided to land on the bay outside a small settlement which was dry of water due to low tide. If the weather did not improve, it was my intention to taxi into the settlement at high tide for overnight shelter. Several small islands formed a natural harbour for this small place which was not indicated on my map. I figured it was probably a winter settlement where the inhabitants went to the outer islands for the summer months to fish, returning for the winter hunting. By drifting and taxiing around, we killed a couple of hours waiting for the tide which appeared to be high enough around early afternoon. We taxied into the small harbour and soon realized that it was, indeed, deserted, and with the wind freshening and blowing on the settlement, I felt my small aircraft anchor would not hold the aircraft should we have to stay overnight. I therefore taxied to the northeast shore which had a sandy/muddy area with long weeds growing, and which was protected by a growth of low, stunted fir trees.

I taxied into the sandy area until the aircraft grounded on its hull. I took the anchor out of its nose storage area, opened the windshield door, threw the anchor into the bushes and secured the anchor line to the nose cleat. It was now about 1800 hours, and as the tide was high I figured the following morning we should have another high tide around 0600 hours, at which time — assuming the weather cleared — we would take off and be in Harrington Harbour in ten minutes or so.

The aircraft had a small can of emergency rations, a sleeping bag, and an axe. We also had a lunch which had been prepared for us by the nurse at the nursing station in Flower's Cove. Just before dark, I put on my long rubbers and walked around the small bay to the settlement and picked some berries which I brought back to the aircraft in a can I had found in one of the houses. The water level was noticeably lower on my return, with the aircraft almost high and dry. I secured the flight controls and stowed the pilot and co-pilot seats in the nose section, laid out the sleeping bag, and the three of us spent a very fitful night.

At 0600 hours it was clear, the wind blowing strong from the west and not a bit of water to be seen. From our position tucked inside the little bay, we could see only the two islands at an oblique angle. The little harbour was absolutely dry. Where was my high tide? I had assumed tides were normal on this coast, but now realized that maybe the area had only one high tide a day, possibly caused by the restrictive action to the tidal flow at the Strait of Belle Isle. That being so, we probably would not get clear of the sand bank into which we were solidly grounded until late afternoon! We discussed the situation and felt a top priority was to turn the aircraft around, so that as soon as we were partially floated we could start the engine and power the aircraft off the muddy/sandy bank on which we rested.

We installed the two seats, rolled up the sleeping bag, and ate a few berries. I opened the windshield door and, instantly, the wind blew it clear of my grip and smashed it violently against the windshield, cracking it into five pieces! Great! I'd never flown an aircraft with no windshield.

The immediate problem was to turn the aircraft around. I had considered starting the engine and reversing the propeller but decided there would not be sufficient thrust. I retrieved the anchor from the woods, cut several trees and limbed them, and using them as levers under the keel, we attempted to pry the aircraft around. It was useless. With the V-keel of the hull mired in the muddy sand, it was a fruitless effort. We would have to wait for some water buoyancy.

All that day we anxiously waited for the tide to come in. Finally, at mid-afternoon, we could see the water glistening in the sunlight inside the islands! Slowly it crept nearer and nearer to the aircraft. My one anxious thought was: Will the tide be high enough to float the aircraft sufficiently to allow us to turn it around? In the meantime, I'd removed all the broken pieces of perspex in the windshield frame and had stored them in the baggage compartment.

By 1900 hours the water was beginning to float the aircraft. Now was the time to try to turn it around. With the help of the two Patey's — one on each float, up to their knees in water and mud — and me using a tree trunk under the forward keel, we gradually turned the Seabee around, facing the open water. We were ready!

We started the engine, did a quick check of everything, lowered half flap, and opened the throttle. We gradually started to slide forward; then with a little drop, we were off the mudshelf and freely floating. I taxied outside the islands, and with the whole of Aylmer Sound ahead, opened the throttle to take-off power. What a pleasure to feel the aircraft respond, as though she was as anxious as we were to get airborne! Surprisingly, there was hardly a breeze in my face from the open windshield. I suppose that with the forward speed the air in the cabin compressed and thereafter the airflow passed over the nose, almost as if the windshield were there. We climbed over the point of land separating us from Harrington, and in ten minutes had landed and tied up at the IGA dock near the hospital. Everyone there was a little anxious, as they had been advised by the nursing station in Flower's Cove that we had left the previous morning and were wondering what happened to us.

The following morning, with the use of a drill and 1/16"

bit, I placed the pieces of windshield perspex together, laced them with copper wire, and inserted the repaired windshield into the rubber framing of the windshield opening and taped it in place with adhesive tape. Our departure and flight to St. Anthony was made later that day without incident and in good weather.

Don and I departed St. Anthony at 0800 hours the next morning and landed at Baie Verte at 0920 where we picked up Mr. Muir and his daughter once again, and left immediately for Gander to refuel. Of course, everyone was anxious about our delay and the broken/repaired windshield. During the flight to Gander, I noticed through the wing mirror that the tail section was a little darker than usual, caused by leaking oil from the propeller head. We were passing over Brighton at the time and I decided to land and replenish the oil tank. This we did, and after getting some automotive oil from the local merchant, we were airborne once again and landed at Gander airport at noon.

We had lunch in the terminal restaurant while the aircraft was being refuelled and the tail cleaned by our maintenance people. We departed Gander at 1400 hours and landed Torbay airport at 1520 hours. Mr. Muir thanked me for a most interesting flight and suggested I have the seal in the propeller hub replaced. I had explained to him that the O Ring seal in the actuating cylinder in the propeller hub was leaking oil resulting in the oil smeared on the tail section.

Incidently, the repaired windshield was on the aircraft for the next three weeks, until a new one arrived from the factory!

"WHALE SPOTTING"
AUGUST 31 – SEPTEMBER 1, 1949

I received a call at my home in St. John's from EPA's Managing Director, Eric Blackwood, requesting me to fly the Seabee to Twillingate and pick up Captain Arnie Borgen and take him whale spotting. Captain Borgen, a Norwegian, operated a whaling company out of Williamsport on the northern peninsula. They had run out of whales and he wished to see if he could spot any new herds from the air. As he wished an early start the next morning, I decided to fly to Twillingate that afternoon and overnight there.

I departed Torbay airport at 1515 hours and landed Gander at 1625, refuelled, and was off to Twillingate at 1700. The weather outlook was good, with the forecaster optimistic that I would enjoy good conditions over the water east of Fogo Island the next day. We landed Twillingate after a forty-minute flight, secured the aircraft on a mooring near Ashborne's Wharf, and walked to the Harbourview Hotel where Captain Borgen was to meet me that evening.

Captain Borgen arrived early in the evening and we discussed a flight plan for the morning. He wished to explore the area from the Funk Islands to a point fifty miles east, then take a direct line to St. Anthony — a flight of 250 miles. As I could refuel in St. Anthony, I had sufficient range for the flight. The fact that the planned flight was virtually all over water in a single-engine aircraft bothered me a bit; however, the Seabee is amphibian, so we could land on the water if forced to.

After breakfast at 0700 we walked to the wharf, and used a small boat to get out to the Seabee. After tying the boat to the mooring, I started the aircraft engine and taxied clear. With calm winds we took off out the harbour and turned east towards Fogo Island. The time was 0810. Captain Borgen thought the spotting would be most effective from a height of 500 feet, where I levelled off and settled down for the forty-five minute flight to the tiny Funk Island. Visibility was excellent. And the Funk Islands were visible from forty-five miles as we passed over Joe Batt's Arm in Fogo. Captain Borgen began sweeping the area with his binoculars and was spotting a few Finback whales. He was very excited, and seemed to be enjoying himself. After we passed over the Funk Islands, Captain Borgen thought another half-hour on an easterly course would be sufficient, then we'd turn to the northwest towards the Grey Islands, and then on into St. Anthony to refuel.

About twenty minutes out of Funk, the serenity of the flight was shattered as — suddenly — the engine made a series of bangs which were actually cut-out / cut-in / cut-out / cut-in! I checked the instruments for some cause of this malfunction: fuel was no problem and all temperatures and pressures looked normal. My passenger looked extremely alarmed, as I am sure I must have. I advised him we would have to land, as we were — even then — losing altitude due to loss of power. The sea looked reasonably smooth with a slight swell moving east to west, and I was confident I could land with no problem. I was resigned to this when, for no reason, the engine began running smoothly again.

I had already turned the Seabee towards Fogo Island with the intention of getting as close to land as possible; unfortunately, the aircraft was equipped with only a short-range radio with a capability of fifteen to twenty miles for communication to the airport control towers, and operated on a different frequency than that used by marine. With the engine running smoothly again, I started a slow climb, hoping to gain a little altitude before it acted up again. After about ten minutes — sure enough — the problem began again. It seemed as though the engine would stop / start / stop / start momentarily and then resumed firing. This would go on for ten to fifteen seconds, then run normally for several minutes.

I told Captain Borgen I intended to proceed on to Gander where maintenance would be available. He agreed. By this time we had both settled down and were prepared to accept the inevitable ditching. The engine continued to miss intermittently; however, it always regained sufficient power to gain back the altitude we had lost when it was malfunctioning. The shoreline of Fogo finally passed below us and I considered whether or not I should land at Joe Batt's Arm or continue on to Gander. There was no assistance and facility available at Joe Batt's which could fix our problem, so we decided to continue on. We changed course for the fifty mile flight to Gander. Meanwhile, I was trying to make contact with Gander control tower to advised them of our problem and possible ditching. During the last hour we had managed, between stoppages, to gain an altitude to 1000 feet and were feeling a little more comfortable with the situation.

Over Carmenville, we finally contacted the Gander control tower and advised of our situation and that we were planning to land there, and asked them to alert our office. The airport was now visible and I prepared to land. Although the engine had not missed for the last twenty minutes or so, we let out a sigh of relief when the wheels touched the runway!

I thanked Captain Borgen for his understanding and expressed my regret that we could not complete his flight as planned. He seemed, nevertheless, content that he had spotted some whales in the Funk area, but as far as I know, he did not repeat the exercise!

Our maintenance worked on that engine for weeks with no luck. I test-flew it at least three times, but it was always the same. They finally sent the engine to Montreal for a complete overhaul. We were later advised that our problem was burnt and deformed intake and exhaust valves, probably caused by using poor quality fuel and running at too high temperatures. This was understandable, as many times in the early days it was necessary to use a low-octane fisherman's Acto gas, since aviation gas was not available.

"POLIO CASE"
November 2, 1949

We had received a call from the Department of Health to dispatch an aircraft to Burin to evacuate a polio case to St. John's. Nurse Carter, who was to be the escort for the patient, arrived Torbay airport at 0800 hours and we were airborne shortly thereafter. This was the first reported case of polio since a spate of them some weeks before. With a strong easterly wind and a grey sky, we passed over Conception Bay and down over the islands of Placentia Bay with a good groundspeed, landing in Burin after a one hour, fifteen minute flight. I picked up a boat mooring in front of the Burin Cottage Hospital, where a boat soon arrived with a young patient, Joseph Dicks, on a stretcher.

We accommodated the stretcher case by lowering the back of the forward passenger seat and laying the patient fore and aft on that and the right-hand side of the rear seat. The nurse then sat on the left-hand side of the rear seat and was able to attend her patient. We were airborne at 1000 hours and set course for St. John's into a stiff east wind with light rain.

The flight to St. John's took fifteen minutes longer than the flight to Burin, with visibility reduced at times in rain, which can be bothersome in a Seabee without a propeller slipstream to help keep the windshield clear. There was no defogging system available, so a small rubber-bladed fan was used for demisting purposes, which helped a little. An ambulance met us at Torbay airport, into which the patient was transferred.

Twenty-five years later, on a flight to Wabush, Labrador, in a Boeing 737 jet, the senior flight attendant came forward and said, "Captain Jones, there is a Mr. Dicks on board who would like to visit the cockpit."

I said, "Certainly; send him forward."

The young man turned out to be the same Joseph Dicks

whom I had flown from Burin to St. John's as a patient years before, left slightly crippled as a result of the polio, but otherwise healthy and now a successful businessman in Wabush.

"A WINTER FLIGHT"
January 22 – 23, 1950

EPA's fleet of aircraft, beginning January 1, 1950, consisted of one Norseman, one Stinson Station Wagon, one Cessna Crane, and one Seabee. The Seabee had never been designed to be used as a skiplane in northern temperatures; however, out of necessity, we nevertheless decided to use it as such for carrying mail to northern points.

The main wheels were replaced by Federal metal skis and the wing floats were removed. A blowpot and two sections of six-inch funnelling and an elbow were used as the system to heat the engine during cold temperatures. The blowpot rested on top of the hull, with the funnels resting on the blowpot and running into the engine cowling below the propeller hub. It worked, after a fashion, but required constant attention. Unfortunately, the engine didn't have oil dilution and, because of its location on top of the wing and fuselage, it was difficult and messy to drain the oil for preheating. The cabin had no heat, and this was very uncomfortable inasmuch as — besides the occupants freezing to death — all the windows frosted over, at times leaving the pilot with nil visibility. Because of this, I kept a small, wet bag of salt on hand, and by rubbing this on the windshield, I would be momentarily given visibility until the windshield glazed over again. As a last resort, I could always open a small perspex panel in the forward left side window and, with a blast of cold air in my left eye, see a little of what was ahead! Under these crude conditions, I operated the aircraft during the month of January, 1950, until the arrival of our new DeHavilland Beaver.

The first portion of the flight was a routine mail flight to La Scie, ninety miles north of our winter base at Millertown Junction. It was at this point that the post office had established the winter mail service, with EPA being the contractor for the air deliveries to all points north. With four hundred pounds of mail and a Norseman starter on board, we were airborne at 0700 and climbing to the north, crossing over the dazzling white topsails, Green Bay, and on into La Scie where we used the frozen surface of Stake's Pond for our winter operations.

The mail was passed over to the mail courier, and two of our maintenance staff, Bill Harris and Wally Dier, boarded for a flight to Roddickton on the northern peninsula where our one and only Norseman was down with an unserviceable starter. Bill and Wally had been in La Scie for two weeks, working at salvaging a Cessna Crane which had been damaged in a landing the year before. They had installed replacement landing gear and propellers; then, the day previous, Hank Hicks had crashed it on its test flight. Hank was ok, but the aircraft had been demolished.

Take-off from the pond was routine and we headed northwest over the waters of White Bay, Horse Island, and Englee. The windows frosted up badly, making it necessary to apply my wet salt-filled bag so we could have some visibility. Over Roddickton we circled, trying to see where the Norseman was parked — but to no avail. We landed on the harbour ice which had a rough coating of snow on it, and parked near the post office where a layer of green fir boughs were laid out to keep the skis from freezing onto the ice. Fred Clouter, our agent, met us, and our first question was: "Where's the Norseman?" Fred told us that Jack Barton, the pilot, had it covered over in the corner of Saunders & Hounsells' premises, and had the engine out on a tripod.

"What?," asked Bill.

"Yes," said Fred, "Jack has the engine all ready for the new starter."

Bill and Wally were fit to be tied, as it was not necessary to remove the engine from the aircraft in order to change a starter; it could be accomplished through an access door under the instrument panel in the firewall. What had been planned to be an hour's work could now take a couple of days!

As Bill, who was our Chief Engineer at that time, was needed back in St. John's and could not spare the time now required for the fix, it was decided that Wally would stay and get the Norseman serviceable and return to Millertown Junction with it. Bill and I tookoff the following morning and headed back to La Scie, where we picked up Hank Hicks and some return mail, arriving at Millertown Junction about noon. Bill and Hank went on to St. John's that evening on the train. The Norseman arrived from Roddickton the next day, flown by Jack Barton with Wally Dier as his crewman.

On January 25th I flew the Seabee for the last time that winter, into St. John's, landing on Quidi Vidi Lake as there was no suitable landing area for skis at Torbay airport.

I was checked out on our new DeHavilland Beaver CF-FHS the next day by Eric Blackwood, who had just arrived with it from Toronto. What a beautiful aircraft to fly after a month on the Seabee!

STINSON 108-3 STATION WAGON

This four-place high wing monoplane was powered with a 165 hp Franklyn engine. It was equipped with floats, wheels or skis and cruised around 105 mph.

I flew this aircraft (CF-GPH) a number of times in the late summer/fall of 1949.

Two flights stand out in my memory of this aircraft. The first being on September 12 when I was assigned to transfer a small survey party from Aquaforte on the southern shore of the Avalon Peninsula to Grand Beach on the Burin penin-

Stinson Station Wagon CF-GPH
Taken in the winter of 1951 at Millertown Junction
Anson CF-GSA in background

sula. The flight was quite routine and the transfer from Aquaforte to Grand Beach was carried out with no problem whatsoever. After landing the party at Grand Beach I took off for Quidi Vidi in St. John's. Shortly after take-off the engine started running rough. However as I was alone I elected to continue the flight rather than land with no help available maintenance-wise until I reached base.

I was about thirty minutes airborne when the power faded to the point where I had to land. The island near Great Paradise Placentia Bay seemed to provide the best shelter so I put the aircraft down and taxied to a small beach where I grounded the back of the floats, got out my small tool kit and opened the engine cowl to see if I could spot the trouble. I found the left-hand intake manifold hanging off, several nuts were missing, the others quite loose. I tightened the nuts which were loose and started the engine. However it still ran rough due to air leakage around the gasket.

Some fishermen in a motor boat had seen me land and they had come to see if I needed any assistance. They offered

Stinson Station Wagon CF-GPH on floats
Marsh Jones at the controls

to go to Great Paradise and see if they could get me a few nuts to replace the ones that were missing.

They returned after a half-hour and fortunately the nuts they had obtained were acceptable.

I started the engine which now sounded normal, eased the aircraft from the beach and took-off for St. John's with no further problems.

Another flight I remember with the same aircraft was on September 28 when I was assigned a flight to pick up a small child with polio at the hospital in Channel.[3] A nurse Normore was to go along to accompany the patient. After a three-hour flight in deteriorating weather, we landed at Channel into a strong southwest wind, and taxied in and tied up to a wharf near the hospital. The nurse left me to walk to the hospital but returned shortly and informed me the patient was at Rose Blanche, about eighteen miles east of Channel.

We took off and headed east to Rose Blanche which we were over in fifteen minutes, looking down on a open harbour with long white wind streaks and swells rolling in from the Gulf of St. Lawrence. I knew the landing was going to be rough as there was no protection from the open sea. However, due to the nature of the flight, we felt we should give it a try.

I lowered full flaps and brought the airspeed back to 65 mph and, using lots of power, made a slow engine-assisted approach. I made a soft touchdown and pulled off the power. However we were smack into a high swell which we struck with a heavy impact. I heard a sound like a rifle shot and thought Oh God! The undercarriage is collapsing!!

After another small bump we were stopped and everything seemed normal so — with some difficulty — I turned the aircraft and taxied downwind into a small cove and the inside harbour. I tied up alongside a motor boat and inspected the float struts and rigging. I found a diagonal rigging wire had snapped during the landing, causing the "rifle shot" sound. This damage would have to be repaired before we could take-off!

Nurse Normore was informed that the polio patient, a two-year-old child named Edwards, was at Harbour Le Cou and that it would take several hours before they would arrive. In the meantime the weather had deteriorated further, and,

---

3   Near Port aux Basques on Newfoundland's southwest coast.

considering the damaged undercarriage, I decided to stay overnight hoping for an improvement.

I made use of the few remaining hours of daylight to remove the broken rigging wire and with some strong fisherman's net line, using diagonal laps from float fitting to fuselage fitting, managed to strap the undercarriage so the effect was a satisfactory (though temporary) repair.

The following two days saw dense fog cover the entire south coast making flying impossible. However as the weather for October 1 looked promising, nurse Normore had the patient brought to Rose Blanche so we could have an early take-off.

The morning of October 1 dawned calm and clear so we were airborne bright and early for St. John's.

After two hours the ceiling started to lower to the point we had to land and sit for a hour at Bellevue Beach, Trinity Bay. We took-off again and landed due weather at Manuels, Conception Bay, where after a short delay we were able to take-off once again and this time managed to reach our destination of Quidi Vidi Lake in St. John's.

This visual flying is really for the birds. However in those days with very limited instrumentation and facilities there was really no other choice!

Chapter 4

The Airmail Service

The winter airmail service was awarded to EPA effective January 1, 1950.

As our aircraft had to operate from a snow or ice surface, due to being equipped with straight ski arrangement, it was decided to operate from Joe Glodes Pond, Millertown Junction, which was a few miles north of Buchans and on the main Trans Newfoundland Railway. A post office holding depot was built and this served the service well until the base was moved to Gander after the 1953 winter season. This move was made primarily because of the new wheel/ski arrangement available which allowed the aircraft to take off from the dry runways at Gander and land at the coastal settlements on

Norseman CF-GMP at Roddickton, White Bay, 1950

the snow and ice with the skis lowered below the wheels.

During the first winter season mail was delivered on a weekly schedule to the Green Bay and White Bay area, the northern peninsula and southern Labrador as far north as Cartwright. The service was expanded over the years to include North Labrador points as far as Hebron and all of Notre Dame and Northern Bonavista Bay. In all about forty-three points were eventually served. The post office had hired mail couriers at all points who generally doubled in base as EPA agents, who were responsible to ensure the ice was thick enough to bear the aircraft weight, and to mark the checked area with the green tops off small trees.

About 103,000 lbs of mail were delivered during the first winter and the figure generally increased by 50,000 to 100,000 lbs each additional year to a point where, in 1958/1959, over 800,000 lbs were delivered. When space was available, passengers were carried at a unit toll and parcels of express (generally liquor) were also carried.

At the start of winter 1950, EPA's fleet consisted of one Stinson Station Wagon CF-GPH, one Republic Seabee CF-GPF and one Norseman CF-GPM. EPA's first Beaver, CF-

Norseman CF-GPM, Beaver CF-FHS and Norseman CF-QAA
at Millertown Junction Winter Airmail Base

FHS was placed into operation on February 2 when I flew it to Gander Bay for a patient for Gander Hospital. Thereafter the Beaver was used primarily for hospital flights and mail when it was available.

The mail service was, in our opinion, carried out quite satisfactorily and to a reasonable degree of reliability. The service was operated under visual flight rules, day only, and with very little weather information available and — in the early years — without the use of radio communication. Pilots literally flew by their eye balls and when the weather became too much they landed and sat it out. The aircraft were well equipped for such a contingency and the pilots were very resourceful.

There would always be a public element who could not understand if the weather where they were was good, why the mail plane could not get through. The post office received a telegram at one point from Bob Gillard at Englee, White Bay which went roughly as follows "If the eagle that lifted Sinbad out of the valley of death had the mail contract it would do a better job than EPA." As it happened I was able to fly into Englee the following day and explain to Mr. Gillard that the weather at our base was far different from Englee, preventing us from take-off. The post office determined the mail schedules. However, with the great quantities of mail available for certain points — St. Anthony for example — it was necessary to dispatch additional flights over and above those required by the schedule.

Generally if the west coast from Daniels Harbour to Flowers Cove — four points — was scheduled for Thursday, one aircraft would do the schedule with northern letter mail for all points, with additional aircraft loaded with bulk parcel mail for single or multiple points. Actually when the weather was flyable the mail planes were always in the air.

Maintenance on the aircraft was done between flights or when the weather was bad. Everything was done outside in the weather. The aircraft were always parked with the skis on a bedding of green boughs or several logs so the skis would not freeze on, and permanent tie downs were frozen into the ice to secure the aircraft from moving in the wind. Snow was generally brushed off the wings, or sawed off using a length of rope. Engine covers were always used and the engine heated by a Herman Nelson (gasoline fired) heater.

The Norseman and Beaver aircraft engine had an oil dilution system available which helped tremendously in very cold weather as it thinned the oil, reducing the drag in the engine which allowed it to turn over faster on startup.

I remember one time returning from a flight with a Norseman to Millertown Junction. After the engine had cooled sufficiently, I started the engine and diluted the oil for about five minutes, which was sufficient for the amount of oil in the tank and the anticipated temperature. I shut down the engine, then left the aircraft and went to the staff house for the evening.

The next morning the aircraft was loaded with mail and engine started and warmed up and ready to go when I arrived. I taxied out on the lake to the take-off area, turned into the wind, did my take-off check and opened the throttle. I was airborne and over the shoreline of the lake when the windshield turned black. I immediately pulled down the side window, looked out and got a faceful of oil. I pulled my head back and looking diagonally forward, I turned down wind and circled to the left. I lowered the landing flaps and with some difficulty managed to land and taxi back to the parking area where I shut down the engine. When I jumped out of the cabin I was met by Cyril Ivemy, our aircraft mechanic, who enquired "What's the problem?"

I pointed to the oil all over the cowl and frontal area of the Norseman. "I think I've blown the oil dilution. How long did you let the engine sit before you restarted it this morning?" I asked.

"About twenty minutes" he said "and I only diluted her five minutes last night!"

"In that case she has had double dilution as I gave her five minutes before I went to dinner last night" I replied.

"In that case" he responded "You blew every bit of diluted oil out through every seam and joint in the engine."

Fortunately I had managed to return and land quickly so there was still sufficient oil remaining in the engine, and no damage was caused by the incident, however I made sure in the future that there was no misunderstandings relating to who did the oil diluting!

Recap of Operations 1949 — 1950

During the period of June 1949 to December 1950 EPA's activities were many and varied.

The greatest revenue producer was the winter mail service during which 103,000 lbs of mail had been delivered to White Bay, the Northern Peninsula and Southern Labrador together with many passengers plus freight and express. Hundreds of mercy flights had been carried out for the Department of Health, some survey work, general charters and perhaps the biggest summer undertaking, a contract with the Power Corporation of Canada wherein we provided all the air support — using Norseman and Beaver aircraft — required to carry out water power surveys in the Bay D'Espoir, Bay Du Nord and Terra Nova water shed areas.

EPA's involvement meant moving three six-man survey crews — each with three square-stern eighteen-foot freight canoes and equipment — from lake to lake on a weekly basis. Each move required from six to eight loads by Beaver or Norseman. This operation was quite successful and was continued during the summer of 1951.

Aircraft used during the period were one Cessna Crane CF-FDR, one Anson CF-GSA, one Norseman CF-GPM, one

Beaver CF-FHS, one Seabee CF-GPF, one Stinson CF-GPH and one Piper Cub CF-GPD.

Norseman at Pudups Lake, 1950

Personnel:

Executive	E.W. Blackwood, Managing Director/Pilot.
Office Manager	Elizabeth Holland
Pilots	Marsh Jones
	Don Patey
	Jack Barton (2 months)
	Hank Hicks (3 months)
Maintenance	W.H. Harris, OIC Maintenance
	Jack Phennel, Engineer
	Emerson Blackwood, Helper
	Wally Deir, Engineer
	Cyril Ivemy, Engineer

The Republic Seabee CF-GPF was lost in a violent storm at St. Anthony during the night of October 25 when its mooring lines parted and the aircraft broke-up on the shoreline.

The Cessna Crane CF-FDR was scrapped during May 1950 as it was no longer required in the operation.

Chapter 5

Early Flights: Norseman and Beaver

BEAVER — Memories

The Beaver is an all metal, single engine, high wing monoplane powered by a Pratt & Whitney R985 Junior Wasp engine delivering 450 hp. It accommodates six passengers and pilot or generally handles a 1000 lb payload of freight or mail. It is a very versatile aircraft with short take-off performance and is easily adapted to wheel, skis or floats. Its cruising speed is around 110/115 mph on skis and floats and with the long range belly strap-on tank, which EPA had, could give you a range of 700+ miles. EPA had ten Beavers in operation at one point in 1956. Its construction was such that it was completely salvageable after a salt water dunking, i.e. breaking through weak harbour ice. At one point EPA had three Beavers break through ice on the same day in different locations All were lifted clear of the ice, dried out, and eventually flown back to base.

There are a number of flights using Beaver aircraft which stand out in my memory. My first flight to Labrador on February 14, 1950 was memorable not only because it was to Labrador, but I had recently been checked out on this delightful aircraft which was real comfort after the Seabee which I had been flying during January.

It was a glorious winter day with everything white on the coastline of Labrador as I flew north with mail stops at

Beaver CF-FHS amd Marsh Jones
Winter of 1950 at Millertown Junction

Forteau, Red Bay, Henley Harbour, Mary's Harbour, Port Hope Simpson, then back across the Strait of Belle Isle to St. Anthony where I refuelled and spent the night. The next morning I loaded three drums of aviation gas to establish a cache in Port Hope Simpson for future flights.

From Port Hope Simpson I flew overland to Cartwright paying close attention to the terrain to see where it could be identified on my map, as it had vast areas marked "Unmapped."

At Cartwright I was met by Dave Massie, the Hudson Bay Manager, who also doubled as the post master. He took my mail then helped me refuel from a drum of gas which he had brought out on the ice on his Komatik.[1] He was assisted by one of his sons, Ian, who in 1953 joined EPA as a mechanic helper and later became one of our senior bush pilots.

On the return flight I landed again at Port Hope Simpson

---

1 Dogsled.

Early Flights: Norseman and Beaver   39

where Jacob Penney had a passenger and some return mail for me. Then on to Henley Harbour, St. Anthony, Roddickton and Millertown Junction, which was our winter base and winter mail holding point. There were several passengers at the base for Gander and I was needed in St. John's for the following morning, so without delay I was refuelled and, after a stop at Gander, landed on Quidi Vidi Lake in St. John's at dusk. I had made seventeen stops since I'd left Gander the morning before and had flown twelve hours.

My next day flight ended up at St. Anthony overnight where the following morning I landed mail at Port Hope Simpson, refuelled and flew on to Hopedale where an old school friend, Earl Bazil, assisted me in refuelling. Earl was then the Marconi operator there. This was Hopedale's first winter mail delivery by air.

March 12 to March 16, 1950

Just prior to this period the radio station at Battle Harbour in south Labrador was burned out, requiring replacement of all its radio equipment. Canadian Marconi asked EPA if we could fly the new equipment into Battle Harbour and land it close to the station. They reported that a marsh area behind the station had quite a bit of snow on it and their people there thought it suitable for a ski equipped aircraft to land and as such had marked it with red flags.

The radio equipment subsequently arrived in Gander where it was arranged in seven Beaver loads. The equipment consisted of large cabinets, transmitters and receivers.

My first flight, on March 12, was non-stop to Battle Harbour. The weather was clear and cold with a light westerly wind and took three hours and twenty minutes flying time. The landing area looked smooth with a dog sled track running its full length of a quarter mile. I circled several times and then landed, coming to a stop in front of a number of people who had turned out to watch the first aircraft to land on Battle Harbour Island. A Mr. Bradley arranged the unloading of the radio equipment, after which I was quickly airborne and landed at Roddickton to refuel for the flight to Gander.

During the next four days I completed six more flights without incident. My respect for the Beaver and its performance was growing.

March 22, 1950 — Mail to Belle Isle

The post office had heard through the light keeper on Belle Isle that I had landed on Battle Harbour. He asked the post office if they would explore the possibility of having the mail plane try a landing on Belle Isle. They were advised that there was a suitable area on the eastern tip of the island and they would mark the landing area with red flags.

The Belle Isle mail was normally dropped at St. Anthony where it accumulated during the winter to be delivered by boat with the opening of navigation in the spring.

I arrived at St. Anthony in the early afternoon, after I'd completed a mail run to Harbour Deep, Englee, Roddickton and Main Brook. The mail courier met me with the Belle Isle mail and I took off immediately. It was a clear day and I climbed to 5000 feet where, when over Cape Bauld, I could see Belle Isle quite clearly, like a white rocky lump, completely surrounded by northern drift ice. The distance from that point was about fifteen miles.

The whole island was snow covered, with a glaze of ice which glistened in the sun. It looked very still and seemed completely devoid of habitation. As I descended to the eastern end the lighthouse was visible and just west of it was a sloping snow-covered valley with two red flags marking the landing area. I made my approach over the lighthouse and landed in a westerly direction, up slope, in the snow-covered valley. I stopped the engine and got out of the aircraft and unloaded the bag of mail while waiting for someone to appear.

It was extremely quiet, the only sound was that of the metal around the engine cowl contracting as the engine cooled.

Finally there was an indication of life with a dog barking moving ahead of a komatik and driver. They arrived within ten minutes of my landing and I was greeted enthusiastically by the light keeper who wanted to know what I thought of the landing area. I told him it was ok for the condition prevailing and for the Beaver aircraft, but I would prefer the pond on the western end of the island and asked him if it was accessible by dog team if we landed mail there in the future. He said certainly and would check the ice there and put markings out to identify the pond. I assured him the ice would be ok and that the pond was large enough to take any of the aircraft we were operating. The pond was used on all future landings at Belle Isle. I took off with no difficulty in a easterly direction down the valley and over the lighthouse and landed back in St. Anthony in twenty-five minutes.

Spring breakup occurred May 5 when I flew Beaver FHS and Eric Blackwood flew Norseman GPM — both equipped with wheels — to St. John's via Gander for the changeover to floats.

December 17 to December 22, 1951
First Christmas Mail to Cartwright Labrador

This flight deserves to be remembered because it was the first time Cartwright, Labrador had received Christmas mail before Christmas day. Because CF-FHS, with its straight ski arrangement, was used landing areas would be scarce. The ice was not yet safe in most coastal areas of Newfoundland, and there was very little snow. However the post office was anxious to make this flight. The only real problems were at Torbay and Gander airports where I would have to use the side of the runway where snow had been pushed off during previous snow clearing. The rest of both airports was bare.

With the co-operation of the airport snow-clearing crews we prepared two areas, one at Torbay and one at Gander, and, while those temporary runways proved adequate, they were only a little over the width of the skis. Keeping straight on take-off would be tricky.

The aircraft was loaded with mail and by using a wheel and axle on each ski the aircraft was positioned on the side of runway 26 at Torbay and ready to go at 0700. Mr. Ches Crosbie and Bill Harris were at the airport to wish me a good flight.

I started the engine and when the temperatures were in the normal operating range I ran through the take-off check, called the control tower, who wished me luck and gave me take-off clearance. Fortunately the wind was light and down the runway, which enabled me to stay within the confine of the narrow strip, and I was soon airborne and climbing away to the north and Gander.

Overhead Gander an hour and a half later, the snow strip prepared on the side of runway 27 looked very small. However the tower advised me it measured 2000 feet long by 30 feet wide and cleared me to land. I positioned the aircraft and set it up for a power assisted approach with full flap. With the aircraft hanging on the prop, I touched down, chopped the power and came to a stop within the first 1000 feet.

The Esso refuelling bowser[2] was standing by on the eastern end so, with the aid of the driver on my tail, I turned the aircraft around and taxied back to the bowser.

After refuelling I was airborne once again and climbing to the northeast with an intended course of Gander, across Green Bay, over Partridge Point White Bay, then across White Bay and up the east side of the Northern Peninsula to St. Anthony where the inner harbour ice was safe and an area

---

2 Tanker truck.

had been marked out for me. I chose this route for safety sake as there was open water in the bays and with a single-engine aircraft on skis, open water was no place in the event of an engine failure.

The weather was gradually deteriorating with light snow and lowering ceilings. Over Partridge Point I could barely see across White Bay towards Harbour Deep. I continued across White Bay but had to stay off from the coast as the clouds were touching the hills. With the lower land north of Canada Bay I was able to edge inland slightly and continued on to St. Anthony where I landed on the inner harbour ice, two hours out of Gander.

After refuelling, with the weather getting worse, I decided to tie down the aircraft and stay overnight.

The weather turned into a real storm which prevented me from taking-off until December 21, which dawned bright and clear.

With the help of Garland Patey (Don's brother), I cleaned the snow and ice off the aircraft and started the engine, which did not require any heat as I had diluted the oil prior to shutdown a few days before. After a prolonged warm-up to burn off dilution, I gave the engine a short burst of power and was moving. I taxied to the eastern edge of the marked area, turned into the wind and was airborne after a few bounces off the many hard snow drifts on the surface.

The flight to Cartwright took one hour and thirty-five minutes, with everyone there very happy to receive their Christmas mail.

Dave Massie, the Hudson Bay Manager, had a barrel of gas ready to refuel me, after which we went to his home for a cup of tea and something to eat. After wishing everyone a Merry Christmas I was airborne and winging my way back to St. Anthony where I received a message from Bill Harris informing me that I was to proceed to Millertown Junction, leave the aircraft there and come home by train.

Apparently in the last storm the eastern areas of Gander and St. John's had had rain instead of snow, destroying the temporary snow runways I had used on the way north.

I departed St. Anthony the next morning and had a beautiful flight to Millertown Junction. What a difference in weather from my flight a few days previously on my way north. Everything was white and glistening as I flew down the Northern Peninsula past Englee, Hooping Harbour, Harbour Deep, then a slight course change to take me directly to Joe Glodes pond, our winter base in Millertown Junction.

I landed and taxied into the parking area near the post office and maintenance hut, shut down the engine and proceeded to secure the airplane for a few days.

I hopped the Rail Express that evening and arrived St. John's the following morning December 23 in time for Christmas.

NORSEMAN — Memories

The Norseman was without a doubt a real bush pilot's air-

Norseman CF-GPM at Torbay Airport prior to flight
to Lac-à-la-Tortue, Quebec
to get floats installed

plane. It was extremely rugged and performed well on either floats or skis. It was fairly large with its fifty foot wing span and was capable of carrying close to a ton payload, or seven to eight passengers. It was powered by a Pratt and Whitney R1340, 600 hp engine and cruised on skis or floats at 115+ mph. It had a very strong undercarriage, and it was because of this feature most of the first ski landings at Horse Islands and Grey Islands were carried out by me using the Norseman aircraft. These landings areas were actually marshes or bogs with some flashes of water and stunted undergrowth on them. Then with a sprinkling of snow and frost you had your landing area.

My memories of flights in this aircraft are numerous and unforgettable. I will start with the first flight I made and strangely enough the aircraft CF-GPM was equipped with wheels.

I never did get a formal checkout, but was turned loose for a self-checkout for an hour and thirty minutes with the aircraft on wheels, which I came to eventually realize was the most difficult configuration. Anyway it went off fairly well to the point I was comfortable with it, and was assigned the task of flying it to Lac-à-la-Tortue, in Quebec to have it changed over to floats.

The floats were Edo 7170s and cost EPA $6000.00. A good buy at today's prices. My wife Enid and I decided that this was a good opportunity to have a second honeymoon, (the first one being two days between flights). I tried the idea on Eric Blackwood, who approved it. However he pointed out I could not take any passengers across the Cabot Straight in a single-engine aircraft on wheels. "You'll have to pick Enid up in Sydney." This is what we planned so Enid departed St. John's on June 30 on Trans Canada Airlines for Sydney, where she was waiting when I arrived with the Norseman.

I departed Torbay airport on June 30, 1950 at 0800 and arrived Stephenville airport at 1050 where I was refuelled by

Esso and took-off immediately for Sydney. I'll never forget that flight to Sydney. I passed over Port Aux Basques at 10,000 feet with about three miles visibility in haze and started to come over the water when the engine went into automatic rough. I was sure my compass was in error when finally, after forty-five minutes, St. Pauls Island appeared below me. I became less apprehensive and with only thirty miles to go started a slow descent into Sydney airport, which, since I had no radio, I circled until I received a green light to land.

I managed a respectable landing and taxied in to the passenger terminal below the control tower, parked, shut down and went to look for some fuel and Enid. She had been in the terminal for several hours, and as it was now mid-afternoon and the aircraft had still not been refuelled, we decided to book a room at the Isle Royal Hotel and stay overnight.

After a restful night and having the aircraft finally refuelled we were airborne — with Enid white-knuckled and with a death grip on her seat — heading west to Charlottetown into marginal visual weather. We landed after a flight of two hours from Sydney and decided to stay there the night.

The next morning we went to the airport and checked the weather which looked good all the way to Montreal. While I was doing my preflight inspection of the aircraft I was approached by a gentleman who said "I'm Carl Burke, owner of Maritime Central Airways and Newfoundland Airways." I introduced myself and we chatted for a while during which time he offered me a job with Newfoundland Airways. I thanked him and said I was happy with EPA.

I made and filed my flight plan to Lac-à-la-Tortue with a landing at Fredericton, New Brunswick.

The weather was very good and the landing at Fredericton for fuel was made after a one hour, forty-five minute flight. We refueled and had lunch at the terminal snack bar, and were soon airborne heading west over northern Maine and past Mount Katahdin, which at 5267 feet above sea level was very impressive with its snowy peak. We continued on past Three Rivers and on to Lac-à-la-Tortue where we arrived after a flight of three hours and five minutes. I had never been there before and I was looking for a runway which I could not find. There were a few small buildings that looked like hangers and after a low pass I saw the name "Aircraft Overhaul and Repairs" over one of the buildings. I knew that this is the right place so decided to land. Enid was very apprehensive as she had never landed in an open hay field before, of course I hadn't much experience either. I checked the wind direction and lined up for a westerly approach, held off with power until the edge of the field and touched smoothly in a three pointer in front of the two hangers, taxied in to the front of them and shut down. Art Jarvis, the owner, came out and welcomed us, inviting us to spend the night at his home. He advised me the aircraft would be ready to fly on floats in ten days time.

Aircraft Overhaul and Repair (OAR) was at one time operated as an overhaul and seaplane base by a large paper company who had there a fleet of single-engine flying boats used for fire patrol and surveys. Art Jarvis bought the property from them and set up his own business.

The following morning Enid and I took a bus for Toronto where we spent the next ten days visiting my sister Marjorie and brother-in-law Jim Whiteoak.

We arrived back at Lac-à-la-Tortue on July 14 and sure enough there was GPM on floats at a mooring near the seaplane dock on Lac-à-la-Tortue lake.

Art informed me she was refuelled with full tanks and the wheel gear was loaded. I said we planned to leave the next morning for Shediac, New Brunswick, where we would spend the night and visit with some friends.

The following morning we flew to Shediac, arriving there after a flight of three hours and thirty-five minutes, and

Norseman CF-GPM departing Shediac, New Brunswick
on return flight from Lac-à-la-Tortue

moored the aircraft on a boat mooring at Point Duchesne. I arranged for refuelling and after a great visit with Jean and George Wagg we took off the next morning and — after a flight of four hours and twenty minutes — landed at Millertown Junction. We refuelled from our tank at our winter base and after flying one hour and fifty minutes landed at our summer sea plane base at Bay Bulls Big Pond. All in all a delightful trip. Incidentally our son Rick was born on March 27, 1951.

Chapter 6

Flight Operations — 1951

AVRO ANSON MK 5

*T*his aircraft, powered by two R985 Pratt and Whitney engines was originally designed as twin-engine light bomber but made its niche in aviation as a twin-engine navigational trainer in the British Commonwealth Training plan during World War II! It was of wooden laminated construction and was built by Canada Car and Foundry in Montreal.

EPA's aircraft CF-GSA was used flying mail during the winter of 1951 using a roll on ski arrangement. This necessitated leaving the undercarriage down, resulting in a low

Avro Anson on wheel/skis at Millertown Junction — 1950

cruising speed of 110 mph. I departed Torbay airport for Millertown Junction with this aircraft on January 19, 1951 to support the winter mail service, which was late getting started due to a late freeze up.

I made my first mail flight on January 22 from Millertown Junction with a 2000 lb load for Main Brook and St. Anthony. It was my first experience with a twin-engine aircraft on skis and I was very impressed by the ease of handling as compared with a single-engine aircraft on skis.

Enroute to St. Anthony I thought I'd try and see what it would do on one engine with ski arrangement and full load, so, at a nice altitude of 5000 feet I throttled back the starboard engine to idle thrust and added full power to the port engine. After I had trimmed out the added drag I noticed the airspeed started to decrease to the point where to maintain 90 mph I had to lose altitude at about a hundred feet per minute. Well this was a lot better than a single engine aircraft would do so at least I could greatly prolong the descent if an engine should fail.

I returned to Millertown Junction mid-afternoon.

This aircraft was taken over by Eric Blackwood leaving me with CF-GPH, the Stinson Station Wagon, until the end of February. I did get another chance to fly the Avro Anson on February 18 from La Scie to Millertown Junction after it had received an engine change at La Scie. I was back on the Anson on March 2 and thoroughly enjoyed this aircraft until April 6 when a short flight — which proved to be its last — was made to Flat Water Pond, Baie Verte.

The ice had been deteriorating very fast at our Joe Glodes Pond base in Millertown Junction. On the morning of April 7 Cyril Ivemy, the base engineer, and I walked to the base to inspect the aircraft. It was very foggy and warm. We had two aircraft at the base, Beaver FHS and Anson GSA. All aircraft were sitting in pools of water due to their weight sinking the ice, which was getting rotten and porous.

Flight Operations — 1951

Anson CF-GSA broke through ice at Millertown Junction
April 7, 1851

The ice had been getting bad for several days to this point but the weather east to Gander and St. John's had prevented us from moving the aircraft. I was alarmed to see the extent the ice had deteriorated.

The worst situation was the Anson which was in water a foot deep around its skis. I told Cyril to get in the Anson and start up while I would walk to the east shoreline of the lake and check for better ice. Normally the ice is stronger on the eastern shoreline as the prevailing westerly winds builds up the drifting snow, which eventually forms ice.

I made my way through the fog to the eastern shoreline and was checking the ice with my axe when I heard the Anson's engines increase in power and then silence! In a few seconds I heard "MARSH." I hurried back towards the base and there was the Anson resting on the wings with the undercarriage completely through the ice. Shortly thereafter the forward section of the aircraft sank with only the tail sticking out like the Flukes of a large whale. The aircraft was subsequently written off by the insurance company and sold to Buchans Mining Company for parts as they were operating an Anson on wheels at that time.

Our Beaver and Norseman were flown on skis to Buchans when the weather cleared the next day, and landed on the sand alongside the runway, then changed to wheels and flown to St. John's.

This was the close of the winter operation. However mail flights continued on floats until later in April when open water became available.

Due to poor ice conditions the winter season was not a good one.

Our fleet of one Anson GSA (lost), one Norseman GPM, two Stinson Station Wagon GPH and FQJ and one Beaver FHS had been augmented by the addition of a Norseman CF-DEP wet-leased[1] from Wheeler Airlines in St. Jovite, Quebec. This aircraft, flown by Dorola Theiroux, was a tremendous help in moving the mail for a two month period, as the two Stinsons were generally used at Gander involved in general charter and moving patients on the Notre Dame Bay area.

Approximately 130,000 lbs of mail had been delivered during the season.

Summer Operation — 1951

The Power Corporation of Canada water power survey continued into its second season, and was utilizing either the Beaver or Norseman full time as we were now into drilling of dam sites at the various watersheds. Each camp movement now included drill rods and casing, drill core, air compressors/generators and drills together with the six men, their equipment and eighteen-foot canoes.

As I look at a current map of the area west and northward of Bay D'Espoir the results of the subsequent damming and resultant flooding after the development took place is readily apparent.

---

1 A wet-lease is an agreement to provide aircraft and the pilots to fly them.

Beaver and Norseman at Quidi Vidi Base, St. John's

This operation concluded on September 21 when I moved the last drill crew from Great Burnt Lake to Norris Arm. I then proceeded to Gander where I was advised to refuel and go to Buchans as their Norseman had crashed at South Pond with no reported survivors. In the early evening I arrived Buchans and was briefed by Eric Swanson, Buchans Chief Mining Engineer. He explained that apart from supporting the requirements associated with the accident, it would be necessary for me to support the activities related to their mining exploration program for some time, until they could obtain another aircraft.

The following morning I moved a party from Pebble Pond to Stony Lake and then a party from Buchans to the accident site at South Pond. Eric Swanson, the Royal Canadian Mounted Police and Ministry of Transport were in this party. After landing at South Pond we were met by their camp chief who took us to the accident site. The pilot had been Tommy Matten and the other six occupants had been Buchans Mining Company personnel. There were no survivors as the aircraft had stalled and went nose-in to the ground and burned. A few days later, after the official investigation was completed, I flew the remains of the victims to Buchans in a single box where burial services were held. A memorial cairn was later erected at the site.

The summer operation came to an end with the usual fall hunting camps support flying hunters and game to and from Gander and Newton Pond, Berry Hill Pond, Walls Pond and Little Gander Pond.

On October 10 Mr. Ches Crosbie, our president, called Bill Harris and me into his office and informed us that Eric Blackwood had resigned his position as Managing Director and had sold his shares to Mr. Crosbie. Eric had decided to pursue a career in politics instead of flying. As a result Mr. Crosbie named Bill Harris as Operations Manager and Chief of Maintenance, and myself as Chief Pilot and Head of Flight Operations. With this promotion I would be responsible for all administration of pilot selection, hiring and training; liason with the Department of Transport; responsible for all operational procedures and practices; the Operations Manual and Amendments; flight dispatch and crew scheduling.

Additional personnel added during the year were: Fred Knox, Pilot; Jack Bowdery, Pilot; Ed Lawson, Pilot; Johnny Punt, Mechanic helper; Cyril Jones, Mechanic helper.

Aircraft lost: Anson GSA, through ice.

Aircraft added: Norseman CF-QAA.

Don Patey left the company for a flying job on the mainland.

W.H. (Bill) Harris
EPA Assistant General Manager

Chapter 7

Flight Operations — 1952

Winter Season

The first flight of the season really started on December 17, 1951 when, with Beaver CF-FHS on straight skis, I left St. John's and with stops at Gander and weather delays at St. Anthony, delivered Christmas mail to Cartwright on December 21. The aircraft was left at Millertown Junction on December 22, and I left that evening on the train for St. John's and Christmas at home.

Two of our Norseman — GPM and QAA — together with Beaver FHS were used at Millertown Junction and positioned there for the start of the airmail contract on January 3, 1952. The two Stinsons GPH and FQJ were used at Gander for charter and Department of Health work. The increased capacity was anticipated. Two Norseman aircraft from Wheeler Airlines, piloted by Tom Watt and Howard Kohler, were added to the mail fleet in mid-January. For the first time ever we were in good shape to handle all our flight requirements.

On February 1 I was requested to land mail at Belle Isle in the Strait of Belle Isle. I had landed mail at Belle Isle on March 22, 1950 at which time I used a Beaver FHS and landed in a valley on the eastern tip of the island. This time I was to use a Norseman and land on a pond on the western tip which had been marked with two red flags. I landed mail at

Main Brook and St. Anthony and picked up a bag of mail for Belle Isle.

The flight to Belle Isle took twenty minutes. I circled the pond several times and picked out my landing run into a stiff westerly wind. I could see a glistening glaze on the snow and bare ice patches so I expected a long landing run with no drag on the skis and only the wind to stop the Norseman. I made my approach using lots of power and low airspeed and touched on the snow-drifted surface with a clatter from the skis. The pond seemed very small and I didn't seem to be decelerating at any great speed. Anyway I was committed and the far shoreline was getting closer. Fortunately the shoreline blended into the hillside with hard snow. I literally slid up the smooth shoreline and, with a slight turn by using power and rudder, slid back onto the pond surface and stopped.

There was a box with a hinged top just off the shoreline where I deposited the bag of mail and put the small bag of return mail in the aircraft. There was no sign of any life whatsoever. I started the engine and manage to turn around and taxied back to the east end of the lake, turned into the wind, did the take-off check, opened the throttle and was airborne after a short take-off run.

My return flight took twenty minutes and from then on we continued to make regular stops at Belle Isle.

On my return to base I was advised the post office would now like to try a landing at Grey Islands. The landing would have to be on a marsh behind the settlement as there was no ice to land on. A landing area had been flagged off.

I left Millertown Junction with mail for Harbour Deep, Roddickton, Main Brook and St. Anthony. On return at Roddickton I left all the return mail I had on board there. Picked up the Grey Island mail and with Fred Clouter, our agent and mail courier on board, we were overhead Grey Islands in twenty minutes. As we had lots of snow and frost that winter the marsh area looked reasonably smooth. I made the usual precautionary type power approach and landed. A few small bumps and we came to a stop. No problems. The first airplane landing on Grey Islands.

Ten days later, on February 14, I landed there again with Doctor Gordon Thomas on board to treat and pick up a patient for the hospital in St. Anthony.

Another amusing flight took place on March 20 when it was requested that I pick up the Horse Island mail and try a delivery on a marsh at that place. I left the base with mail for Western Arm, Baie Verte and La Scie. At La Scie I was met by Norm Thoms, the mail courier, who had the Horse Islands mail and a passenger for Millertown Junction. The passenger, Alonzo Noseworthy, who had lived in Horse Island as a child, was taken aback when I told him I was going to try and land mail at Horse Islands. He said "My son you can't pitch a plane at Horse Islands, there is nowhere there to land." I told him I thought the marsh there was suitable and if he wanted to go to Millertown Junction he'd better get aboard!

I strapped him in the copilot seat, started up and took off for the Horse Islands which we were over in twenty minutes.

The marsh looked very good with a heavy layer of snow covering most of the little gulleys and brush.

On the approach I noticed Mr. Noseworthy's knuckles were white and he had a death grip on the seat. The touch-on and landing were quite smooth so I taxied to the east end of the marsh where a small group of people had gathered. As soon as the engine stopped Mr. Noseworthy was out of the aircraft and greeting everyone like old friends, all his apprehension forgotten.

The local merchant made a speech and thanked me for risking my life to get them their mail and in honour of the occasion he presented me with his store calendar.

The take-off and flight back to base were very routine. Mr Noseworthy made the evening train and arrived in St. John's in time for the fisherman's convention.

Marsh Jones and Norseman CF-GPI

On April 25 I delivered a load of mail to Burlington in Green Bay. I taxied in and stopped opposite Thistle's premises and unloaded the mail.

On my return to Millertown Junction I was loaded up once again for Burlington. On arrival there, after a thirty minute flight, I landed, taxied in, and stopped in the same spot I'd used in the earlier flight. The aircraft immediately broke through the ice and rested on the lower fuselage. I yelled to my passenger to get out. I then went back to the main door and started to get the mail out. This was accomplished and assistance soon arrived to help me load empty gas drums in the cabin and under the wings to keep the aircraft from sinking.

I made arrangements with Sid Thistle to cut a channel through the ice and drag the aircraft ashore on its skis.

The aircraft was later salvaged but never flew again due to salt water corrosion in the airframe tubing. This aircraft, Norseman CF-GPI had been my favourite aircraft for winter operation and I was sad to see her go.

Flight Operations — 1952

The winter season came to an end with the fleet having moved to Buchans airport on skis, changed over to wheels then flown to St. John's airport for a changeover to floats for the summer season. The two Wheeler Norseman aircraft left in mid-April for their base in St. Jovite, Quebec. 201,000 lbs of mail had been delivered.

Summer Operations

With aircraft overhauls completed, the aircraft were flown on wheels from Torbay airport to the side of Quidi Vidi lake in St. John's, and there converted from wheels to floats. This took place around mid-May. During this period two of our pilots under training, Doug Moore and Gerry English, who had finished their flying training and obtained their commercial pilot licences were checked out by me on the Stinson Station Wagon on floats. This was part of a training program which we had set up the year before. Its aim was to train Newfoundland pilots to satisfy our future pilot requirements, as we had found that mainland pilots were using EPA as a stepping stone to get a job flying farther west. We felt that by training and subsidizing the cost of training the Newfoundland boys would be inclined to stay with EPA.

Bill Eaton had been our first pilot in this scheme and was presently flying a Stinson Station Wagon. The training to commercial pilot licence had been done by the Newfoundland Flying Club with a Stinson Station Wagon FQJ supplied by EPA. Doug Moore and Gerry English were the second and third pilots, to be followed by Gerry McGrory as the fourth.

It was time to add another Beaver to the fleet.

Bill Harris and I picked up Beaver GBD at Toronto Island Airport Seaplane base on June 25, and flew to Montreal where Mr. Ches Crosbie and a Swedish girlfriend of one of our pilots, Kasper Staufacher, joined us for a flight to Corner Brook via Grand Mere and Fredericton. I dropped Mr.Crosbie and Bill Harris and Alma at Corner Brook and

Inflight photograph of Beaver CF-GBD

docked in front of Bowater Mill. Alma was short taken and after the four hour flight to Fredericton, Alma had to go — which she did immediately she stepped onto the beach. Ches got a great kick out of it!

I then flew to Woody Point, Bonne Bay where I moved a mining exploration crew from Woody Point to Gregory Plateau. This little pond on Gregory Plateau was 1600 feet above sea level and 1200 feet long. It was tight! On my landing run — after a steep sideslip down a hill and firm landing — I stopped right at the shoreline. Exciting to say the least! I completed the job in eight flights and proceeded to Gander.

On July 9 I undertook a very interesting flight. I was requested to proceed to North West River near Goose Bay to pick up a party and fly them to the famous Grand Falls on the Hamilton River.

I stayed at Goose Bay that evening and flew to the ten minutes to North West River the next morning. I was met by a photographer and reporter from *Life* magazine and a guide, Henry Blake, from North West River. They advised me they wished to take pictures of the river bank on top of the falls and wanted me to land as close as possible to the falls. We took off and arrived over the falls after a two hour flight. The falls were visible from a long way, due to the mist rising above the canyon into which the falls dropped. We circled the falls looking for a suitable lake large enough to land on. However there was nothing close by, so we landed on Lookout Lake, about four miles to the northeast. We beached the aircraft and secured it to the trees on the south side of the lake. It was our intention to walk overland to a point on top of the falls. The route didn't look too difficult from the air, mostly low scrubs and the usual stunted trees. There was also a small river which we could follow most of the way.

Around mid-afternoon we arranged our photographic equipment, food and camping equipment into four loads, and set out for the falls. Also, we put on plenty of fly dope, as the black flies were really thick. We could hear the roar of the falls and started towards the sound. The walking was extremely difficult as the ground was not firm but very soft and mossy, and the temperature was 95°F. Our two *Life* magazine people started to complain about the difficulty in walking and the aggravation of the black flies. After two hours we came to a small river which had a large flat rock in midstream on which we rested, and had a lunch and cup of tea.

As it was so hot, and there was some relief from the black flies on the flat rock, we decided to stay there until the evening when it would be better for travelling.

As a matter of fact we did not set out again until 0500 the next morning, after a fitful night trying to sleep and keeping a fire going to discourage the flies. The two *Life* people had sore feet as they had purchased new Logans — without insoles — at the Hudson Bay store in North West River, and we could not help them as we were travelling light and without a change of clothing or footwear. The guide and I did

Marsh Jones standing above Grand Falls
July 10, 1952

double up on the loads we carried to make it easier for them. It was still very hot and we hoped to get to the falls before the sun got too high. This we finally managed to do. As we got closer the roar of the falls was deafening. We followed the little river to its entrance point about 100 yards above the falls. The Hamilton River was a torrent of water as it had a drop of one hundred feet or more on down the Jacopie rapids before it plunged over the 200 foot escarpment into the canyon.

Above the falls we found a shelf built between two trees in which stood two glass jars filled with paper notes. We unscrewed the caps and read the notes, all of which held the names of various parties who had visited the falls over many years. There was one note wherein the party had landed in an airplane on the same lake we had, and gave their impression of the falls and the name of their party. It was dated July, 1928.

After the Churchill Falls power development the two jars were deposited in the museum in St. John's and are available today for viewing by the public. We of course left our note describing our visit and names of our party.

Jerry Cook the photographer took quite a few photographs from different angles and, after he indicated he was through, we packed our gear and set out for the aircraft. In a few hours, after many resting periods, my passengers from New York were ready to pack it in, as they were completely exhausted and could barely walk.

The weather was still well into the nineties and the sky was getting heavy with buildups of large thunderheads. Henry Blake and I had all the gear on our backs and were literally dragging along our two suffering reporters.

After arriving at the aircraft it was not very long before we were airborne and heading towards North West River, dodging thunderstorms all the way. On our arrival there, Doctor Paddon advised me to fly my passengers to hospital in Goose

Bay for immediate treatment. He would advise Goose we were coming and there would be an ambulance to meet us. We took off immediately for Goose and the ambulance took them to the American Hospital for treatment. I stayed there overnight and flew back to St. John's the next morning.

The issue of *Life* magazine published a few months later showed those fantastic pictures of the Grand Falls with no indication of the hardships endured by the two gentlemen responsible for them.

Another significant flight took place on December 23, 1952, when the Christmas mail was flown to Cartwright, Labrador from St. John's, with the aircraft returning the same day.

This accomplishment was possible due to the installation on Beaver CF-FHS of the new wheel-ski undercarriage, allowing the aircraft to use either a dry runway using wheels, or snow using the skis. The skis were hydraulically actuated either through the use of a hand pump or an electro/hydraulic motor.

It was well before sunrise when I departed Torbay airport with Mark Ronayne, a reporter from the *Evening Telegram* on board. Due to strong winds it was necessary to land at Gander airport to refuel. (This was before we installed the long range belly tank to the Beavers which increased our range by 240 miles.) The landing at Cartwright after a flight of three hours, forty-five minutes from Gander was routine with mail and refuelling carried out by Dave Massie of Hudson Bay. Due to strong tail winds we made the return flight non-stop, landing after dark at Torbay airport, three hours, twenty-five minutes from Cartwright.

Following this flight Ed Lawson left the following day in Beaver FHS and made mail deliveries at Rigolet, Makkovik and Hopedale. He managed to deliver the mail but he spent Christmas on the coast.

Flight Operations — 1952

RECAP 1952

BASES
St. John's	Headquarters
Quidi Vidi	Seaplane base
Gander	Deadmans pond -- Winter
	Gander Lake — Summer
Millertown Junction	Winter mail

AIRCRAFT
3 Norseman;	GPM, QAA, GPI (lost Apr 25)
2 Beaver;	FHS, GBD
2 Stinson;	GPH, FQJ
1 Piper Cub;	GPD
2 Norseman;	DEP, FOJ
	(wet-leased from Wheeler Airlines)
	(winter mail operation)

PERSONNEL
W.H. Harris	Operations Mgr
M.B. Jones	Chief Pilot
Elizabeth Holland	Accountant
Jack Bowdery	Pilot
Bill Eaton	Pilot
Ed Lawson	Pilot
Kasper Staufacher	Pilot (summer only)
Doug Moore	Pilot
Jack Anderson	Pilot
Gordon MacPherson	Pilot
Gerry English	Pilot
Jerry McGrory	Pilot

MAINTENANCE
Jack Phennel	Cyril Jones, Helper
Cyril Ivemy	Johnny Punt, Helper
Doug Jewer	

Chapter 8

Flight Operations — 1953

WINTER OPERATIONS

*T*he winter operation of 1953 saw some significant changes inasmuch as Notre Dame Point and Bonavista North Point were added to the mail contract. Operational control for Notre Dame and Bonavista area was set up temporarily in the north bay of Hangar 22 at Gander. Aircraft assigned to the operation were the two Stinson Station Wagons. two Beavers (CF-FHS and a leased Beaver CF-GYP, both on wheel skis), two new Beavers (CF-EYQ and CF-EYW) were added the late winter months. Our Stinson

Beaver on wheel/skis

GPH was lost in a landing accident at Carmanville when pilot Bill Eaton lost control during a crosswind landing on glazed ice. The aircraft was written-off. At Millertown Junction three Norseman GPM, QAA, and HAD (leased) together with Beaver GBD all on straight skis provided support for the mail and charter. During the winter mail delivery totaled 444,854 lbs, delivered to forty-three points from the two bases of Gander and Millertown Junction. With an early breakup of ice, the fleet at Gander was changed over to floats by mid-April and the Gander activities continued out of our seaplane base at Gander Lake.

Several flights come to my memory when I think of this winter. The first involving Norseman GPM. I started up on the morning of March 13 with a load of mail for Western Arm, Baie Verte and La Scie all in White Bay. During taxi-out for take-off position I noticed there was a layer of thin ice with water between it and the main ice. Apart from noticing that the skis broke this layer as I taxied, I paid no further heed to it. When in position for take-off I carried out the take-off check, magneto check, lowered take-off flap and proceeded to take off. Everything seemed normal until shortly after becoming airborne the aircraft felt very tail heavy. I immediately adjusted the trim and continued to climb but requiring additional nose-down trim to the point I had almost maximum trim applied. I decided to continue the flight, as apart from the trim required everything else seemed normal. I figured the mail loaders had loaded some unusually heavy mail sacks into the rear of the cabin which I would adjust after my first landing at Western Arm, a thirty minute flight. After landing at Western Arm and taxiing in to where we unloaded the mail, I got out, went back to the door and started to unload the mail, as I was anxious to see what was causing my problem. The mail courier tapped me on the shoulder and pointed to the tail section of the Norseman. All the fabric on the rear lower fuselage and the lower left tailplane was gone and the area in front of the rudder post was packed solid with frozen slush. No wonder she was tail heavy! On take-off at Millertown Junction the skis had broken through the thin ice which was as sharp as glass, then the propeller slipstream had blown it into the lower fuselage and left tailplane, stripping off the fabric and blowing the slush and ice into the tail post where it immediately froze.

I chopped most of the ice away with my axe and as I had unloaded about 400 lbs of mail I decided to take off. If everything was manageable I could continue my mail delivery. This I did, and since the airplane was performing reasonably well I continued on to Baie Verte and La Scie. The airplane was the focus of some attention at both places and particularly so when I landed back at base. Fortunately I was the only Norseman to use the pond that morning and the condition had rectified itself by late evening.

The fabric was replaced that afternoon with the use of heat from a Herman Nelson Heater and a tarpaulin to contain the heat, and while the new fabric repairs looked rough, they nevertheless got us through the winter.

The second flight I remember that winter was actually carried out using Beaver EYQ on floats out of our base at Gander Lake on April 23. This was a really urgent emergency flight as the accident victim had had his left arm torn off when caught in the fly wheel of a steam engine in a saw mill in Port Hope Simpson. The young man named Green was carried by dog team to the nearest nursing station, at Mary's Harbour, where nurse Jupp had done all she could for the patient. She then sent out a cable for an airlift. After a two hour, five minute flight from Gander I landed in an open water lead between two large ice sheets immediately outside the harbour. (We were still landing ski planes inside the harbour.) The sun was low in the western sky with less than an hour of daylight remaining. The patient was brought in a boat to the edge of the ice and boarded with his father, Heber Green, in attendance, who had the severed arm packed with flour and wrapped, hoping that a re-attachment could be made at the hospital. We took off immediately and with sufficient fuel on board, thanks to the new long range belly tank, headed south for Gander. The weather was good, and with the Gander authorities notified of the nature of my flight — and that I would be landing after dark on the water at Gander Lake — I received landing clearance from the tower. Our maintenance people were at the seaplane base and had a number of car lights turned on to mark the base location. Actually the visibility was fairly good and I had no problem carrying out the water landing.

The patient was dispatched to the Gander Hospital and airlifted to St. John's the following morning. He subsequently recovered and was fitted with an artificial arm and to my knowledge carried out a fairly normal life.

RECAP WINTER 1953

During the winter 444,854 lbs of mail was delivered to Northern Newfoundland, Notre Dame and Bonavista North areas, and literally hundreds of passengers and patients were flown during the same period.

During late March the two Norseman and Beaver GBD were changed to wheels and flown to Gander before the ice deteriorated. The balance of the winter was carried out by float-equipped aircraft as ice conditions deteriorated rapidly leaving ample open water.

SUMMER OPERATION 1953

During the early summer of 1953 Hanger 20 at Gander was leased from the Department of Transport and renovations were carried out with the construction of offices, operations room and maintenance stores to provide the company with a first class home for our operation in an area (Gander) which would give us a more reliable weather base than St. John's.

Flight Operations — 1953

Quarters for our personnel were provided in the old Gander Inn (bldg 63) and the Eastbound Inn wherein apartments were made which proved adequate until the opening of the new Townsite in 1955. The movement from St. John's to Gander took place in October 1953 at which time all operational and maintenance support was setup in Hanger 20. Office personnel remained in St. John's until the spring of 1954 when Gander became the main operational base and headquarters for the company.

On May 31 I took delivery of our first Cessna 180, CF-FYQ, from Laurentide Aviation in Cartierville, Quebec. The aircraft was a four-place all metal high wing monoplane powered with a Continental 225 hp engine. Delivery was on wheel gear as it was our intention to install the floats off the Stinson we had lost in Carmanville during the winter.

Before setting out for St. John's Ches Crosbie, our president, and I flew to St. Jovite for a meeting with Tom Wheeler of Wheeler Airlines to discus the purchase of a Canso, PBY-5A amphibian, CF-HFL.

I returned Mr. Crosbie to Montreal that same afternoon and departed for St. John's on June 2, with a refuelling stop at Moncton enroute. The flight to base took six hours and twenty-five minutes, at an average ground speed of 160 mph.

The aircraft was subsequently changed over to floats and operated very successfully until it turned over at its mooring on Gander Lake during a storm in late July. The aircraft had sustained damage to one of its floats which had not been reported by the pilot Dave Luke. The float filled with water during the storm and the aircraft capsized. It was salvaged and turned over to the insurance and replaced by Cessna 180 CF-HCJ.

Another addition to the fleet that summer was the DeHavilland Otter CF-GCV. This aircraft carried serial number 2 and was flown to us by Russell Bannock, Sales Director of DeHavilland, who checked me out in St. John's on August 7.

I subsequently checked out Jim Lewington who flew it to Goose Bay where he operated the aircraft on a Canadian Marconi contract until the end of October. Jim returned to us in June 1954 as General Manager.

Our first big airplane a Canso PBY-5A CF-HFL arrived on November 3, 1953 from Montreal flown by Captain Frank Henley, an MCA pilot from Moncton N.B. I had a thirty minute flight with him on arrival and thereafter it was one of my favourite aircraft, although I was not to get a checkout until the following summer, as substantial work had to be done by our maintenance before it would receive its Certificate of Airworthiness.

One more flight of significance was the charter of a C-46 CF-HEI from Dorval Air Transport to move 10,000 lbs of mail from Gander to Goose Bay, Labrador on December 23. We had positioned two Beavers on wheel/skis at Goose in preparation for this mail haul to Hopedale, Makkovik, Postville and Rigolet.

The C-46 was a large twin-engine aircraft owned by Dorval Air Transport and crewed by Co-Owners Joe McElrae and Jack (Pappy) Stafford. It was powered by two Pratt and Whitney R-2800 engines developing 2000 hp each, and grossed out at 48,000 lbs take-off weight. I went along with the aircraft and departure was at 2100 hrs December 23. Our flight plan called for an enroute time of two hours at 8000 feet.

To me, at that time, it was a massive aircraft with a very large cockpit and panoramic windshield. You felt you could walk around with lots of space and not get in anyone's way. Captain "Pappy" Stafford was a large man and his hands were even larger. They completely enclosed the large throttles when he grasped them and moved them forward on take-off.

It was a routine flight until the descent, which was associated with numerous backfires from the engines due to cooling in the low temperature and the high airspeed at decreased power. The crew however took this as quite a natural thing in the low temperature prevailing. After landing, Allied Aviation, a ground handling company under the guidance of Jim Thomas, unloaded the mail and moved it to the hanger where the two Beavers would receive it and deliver it over the next few days to the Labrador Coastal points.

We were airborne within the hour and landed at Gander 0200 hrs.

RECAP 1953
AIRCRAFT ADDED:

BEAVER	CF-EYQ, CF-EYW
CESSNA 180	CF-FYQ (capsized) CF-HCJ
OTTER	CF-GCV
CANSO	CF-HFL (not in operation)

PERSONNEL CHANGE
NEW PILOTS:

Ben Rivard	
Ken Dempster	(summer only)
Jim Lewington	(3 months)
Jack Kielley	
Bev Croft	(summer only)
Al Roach	(summer only)
Dave Luke	(summer only)
Ivan Lemoine	(summer only)
Carl Fisher	(winter only)
Cris Madsen	

NEW MAINTENANCE:

Ches Sparks,	Engineer
George Furey,	Engineer
Walt Rockwood,	Radio
Bill Clifford,	Engineer

Chapter 9

Flight Operations — 1954

Winter Operations

*F*or the first time ever we were equipped with sufficient aircraft and a well equipped and located base for our winter operations, and with the night flying endorsement obtained from the Department of Transport our total available daily flying hours could be extended. The endorsement allowed our wheel/ski equipped aircraft to leave Gander before sunrise and return after sunset.

We started off the winter mail season with one Otter CF-GCV, two Norseman GPM, QAA, four Beaver CF-FHS, GBD, EYW, EYQ, one Cessna 180 CF-HCJ, and one Piper Cub, CF-GPD. Pilots on the operation were Bill Eaton, Ben Rivard, Ed Lawson, Stuart Le Gasick, Doug Moore, Don Patey (had returned), Jack Kielley and me. Maintenance had a number of new people: i.e. Art Wildish, Mike Trainor, Bob Walsh, Norm Sheppard, John Paton, and Bob Briggs. In stores Benny Doyle and Bob Carter. Several new personnel were added to our office and supporting staff: Mel Davis, Barb Nugent, and John Anstey.

The mail base at Millertown Junction was closed out with the full mail support being provided from Hanger 20 at Gander. (The post office building was destroyed by fire that summer.) Thanks to the efforts of Walt Rockwood — who headed up our new Radio and Communication section — we now had a Base Communication Radio, which together with all the aircraft being radio equipped, we had communication over our whole area. In conjunction with this, by using appropriate frequency radio crystals we could communicate with the International Grenfell Hospitals up the coast.

The winter operation was going fine until February 2 when three of our Beavers —FHS, EYQ, and EYW — all broke through the ice on the same day. FHS flown by Don Patey landed on newly formed ice in Forteau, Labrador, and broke through and grounded on the bottom just off the shoreline. The aircraft was submerged up to the wings. She was pulled ashore and after extensive work was flown back to Gander by Bill Eaton on March 5th. EYQ broke through a weak section of ice on Twillingate pond. Fortunately the engine was not submerged and she was drained out and flown back to base two days later. EYW broke through a weak section of ice on a fresh-water pond near Valleyfield, Bonavista Bay on a mail delivery. Fortunately only one ski broke through and — with some excellent local support pilot Ben

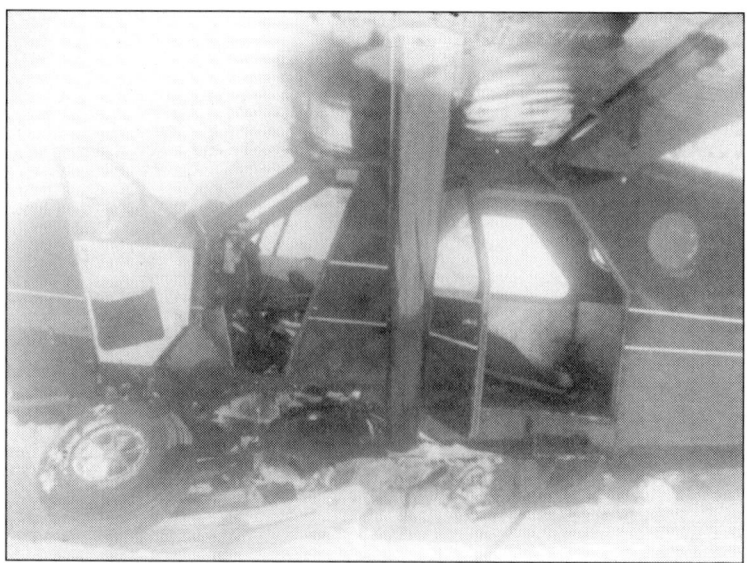

Beaver CF-GBF at crash site

Rivard —managed to raise the ski gear clear of the ice, make a platform and move the aircraft clear. He flew it back to base the same day. Beaver FHS required substantial work plus an engine change due to salt water corrosion. She was out of service for six weeks.

This was not the end of our problems. On February 20 Beaver GBD, flown by Ben Rivard, crashed into the mountains on a mail delivery flight to Parsons Pond and Port Saunders on the west coast. He was flying in marginal weather over the Long Range Mountains and during a turn got caught in a downdraft on the side of a steep snowy slope, and ploughed into the snowy surface breaking the undercarriage.

I was flying south at the time just past St. Anthony when I heard him call and give his position and that he had crashed. He reported to me that he was ok but the aircraft would need a salvage crew with a replacement undercarriage. He advised me the weather was bad and that I should not try and bring in assistance until the weather cleared. I told him I'd be in to pick him up first thing in the morning and would land on the nearest pond to him.

The following morning I departed Gander in Otter GCV with a load of mail for Flowers Cove. Bill Eaton and an aircraft engineer, George Furey, came along to assist and survey the damaged Beaver. We landed our mail at Flowers Cove then flew south to the crash site, which we found with little trouble, located about 200 yards up on a snowy slope from a good size pond which we called Benny's Pond. We landed and while George Furey was assessing the damaged aircraft we lugged the mail down a snowy slope to the Otter. The Beaver was at an elevation of 2000 feet above sea level. After take-off we delivered the Beaver's mail to Parsons Pond and Port Saunders, then returned to Gander.

After consulting with DeHavilland it was decided to build a temporary truss section with undercarriage leg pickups to replace the damaged section. The new section would be bolted in place.

It was March 24 when I flew into Benny's pond again with three of our maintenance people headed by George Furey. With them they had the new truss section with tools, camping gear, provisions, a transmitter/receiver and a small generator. We circled overhead the site and the only part of the aircraft to be seen was the left wing tip, the rest of the aircraft was completely buried in snow. After they had their camp set up and got organized, they carried out the repairs completely inside a snow house dug out around the aircraft. This was necessary due to the continuous drifting snow. We were in daily communication with them and I flew in four more time in the next six weeks. Finally on May 9 the aircraft was ready and down off the slope unto the pond.

I decided I could fly it out and land at Buchans as the ice was bad at the lower levels and the repaired aircraft was on straight skis necessitating a landing on dry sandy ground off the side of the runway at Buchans.

Bill Eaton in the Otter loaded the men and equipment aboard and we both took off for Buchans where a landing was made with no difficulty. We left a crew there to change the Beaver over to wheels and I flew it to Gander the following day. On May 18 I flew it to Toronto where the damage was permanently repaired.

This then was the end of winter operations for 1954.

Total mail delivered was 475,587 lbs.

Summer Operations 1954

I suppose the most significant event was the arrival of A.J. Lewington as our General Manager. Jim had flown our Otter GCV for a period of three months — August, September and October — in 1953, and did an excellent job. We expected great things from Jim and he always delivered. He was a fine gentleman and an excellent man to work for. He had an

Flight Operations — 1954

A.J. Lewington   Roy Cooper

extensive background in transportation both as a pilot and administrator with the Department of Transport before and after the war, and retired from the RCAF as a young Group Captain with three tours of operations in Bomber Command behind him. He had been most recently the transportation officer for Fraser Brace, the contractor who built the Pine Tree radar chain.

Another significant arrival was Roy Cooper who was from Milton, Trinity Bay, and came to us from Maritime Central Airways. Roy had had an excellent RAF record during the war and was credited with being the first person in his squadron to shoot down a V1 rocket.* Roy in my opinion was the most reliable and versatile pilot I had ever hired. I trusted him implicitly in whatever undertaking or aircraft he was to fly. He succeeded me as chief pilot in 1956.

Another pilot who was to become a reliable addition to EPA was Gunner Laurell. Unable to get rid of his Swedish

---

* The V1 rocket was a pilotless explosive device which Germany deployed against England during the latter part of WWII.

Rough conditions on Gander Lake. This picture shows two Beaver aircraft at moorings off from the floating dock.

accent he always called me Morris Yones. He performed yeoman service for EPA, and after we separated our bush operation from our airline operation in 1970 he continued on with the Newfoundland Government, flying Canso Water Bombers — and CF-CRP in particular — to the point where when Gunner retired in the spring of 1988. The Newfoundland Government retired the Canso CF-CRP with him.

Gunner passed away later that year.

Eric Blackwood, the founder of EPA — who had left us in October 1951 — returned as a pilot in June but unfortunately after a few months, due to domestic problems, he decided to move back to the mainland.

Operationally the summer of 1954 was a poor one with continuing poor weather for visual flying activities.

Our usual charter work with the Department of Health, Newfoundland and Labrador Corporation, Public works and Hunting and Fishing kept the aircraft fairly busy when weather permitted.

Fewer hours were flown in 1954 than in 1953 (3478 vs. 3917), however revenues were slightly higher in 1954 versus 1953 ($404,745 vs. $356,382).

Some maintenance construction was done on our Gander Lake docking facility. However, with the continued damage and restricted operations due to rough water conditions, it was becoming evident that we would have to move our marine facilities to Deadman's pond.

The move of our office personnel and records from St. John's to Gander was completed during the summer. Miss Elizabeth Holland, who had been our office manager from the start in 1949, did not make the move and resigned.

Our total personnel for 1954 was 31.

With the appointment of Jim Lewington as General Manager, Bill Harris was appointed his assistant and I was named Chief Pilot and Operations Manager.

Before closing out 1954 I have to mention that Piper Cub CF-GPD was sold to Frank LeDrew in Pasadena as a trade for a 1954 Chevrolet Station Wagon for our use as a company vehicle in our Gander operations. I flew the aircraft from

Piper Cub CF-GPD

Gander to Pasedena on July 6 in two hours and thirty minutes and landed on Frank's farm. Frank and I exchanged documents of the aircraft and the van and I drove the van back to Gander in just over three hours, almost the same time as I flew to Pasadena in the Cub. This was a very nostalgic event for me as I had owned the aircraft from February 8, 1948 until Tuffey and I sold it to EPA in October 1949.

Frank LeDrew later sold the aircraft to a purchaser on the mainland and in looking through an aircraft register some years later I noticed it was operating out of Port Credit, Ontario.

Chapter 10

Flight Operations 1955

1955 was a good year in most respects for EPA. There were a variety of government projects in which EPA participated; i.e. The Mid-Canada Line and Health contract with International Grenfell in St. Anthony. The Mid-Canada Line contract with the Department of Defense production involved two Cansos CF-HFL and CF-HGF (wet-leased) and one Otter CF-GCV. The radar line situated along the 55° parallel of latitude was meant to be a back up for the Distant

Canso CF-HFL
1954

Early Warning line, and construction was to start early in 1956.

It was in this operation that our Canso HFL was to show its value. Flown by Captain Rex Clibbery and co-pilot Bob Packer it performed yeomen services during the summer, outperforming on an individual basis all the other Cansos (about fifteen) participating in the operation. The Cansos were used mainly in the movement of petroleum products in one of its 750 gallon wing tanks. Landings were on lakes at the various sites where the product was off-loaded by gravity flow into forty-five gallon drums positioned on floating docks.

In conjunction with this, the Otter GCV piloted by Benny Rivard provided additional support moving general freight, provisions and personnel from a base at Knob Lake. Ben flew upwards of 550 hours in the three month period that he was

De HavillandOtter

there. He was later relieved by pilot Doug Moore who subsequently finished out the summer contract. The International Grenfell Association — who provided health services in Northern Newfoundland and Labrador through the Department of Health — contracted for one Beaver to be stationed at St. Anthony. This aircraft was flown by Don Ballantyne and showed excellent utilization.

Winter Operations 1955

Most of the fleet was involved with mail during an excellent winter. Unfortunately the Norseman CF-GPM was lost when it broke through the ice in St. Anthony in January and, due to the effect of salt water corrosion of its tubular steel construction, was declared a total loss.

One particular flight stands out in my memory of that winter involving a mail delivery to Labrador in Otter CF-GCV.

On February 28 I departed Gander with Rex Clibbery (our Canso Captain) and a load of mail for Charlottown and Black Tickle in Southern Labrador. A refuelling stop was made at Roddickton and the first mail stop was made at Charlottown, at the head of St. Michaels Bay. With excellent weather we proceeded up the coast to Black Tickle. A circuit was made for ice observation and, as everything looked normal, we landed heading out the bay along the line of tree top markers. During the turn to taxi back to the inner bay after landing, the skis broke through the ice and the aircraft settled on the upper struts of the undercarriage. What a predicament!

Black Tickle is completely devoid of trees and my immediate thought was to build a platform over the area where we had broken through, but what would we use for material?

One of the numerous bystanders suggested that there might be planks in Guy Earl's shed on his fishing premises. I told the man to bring over all the long planks and poles he

Norseman CF-GPM through the ice at St. Anthony
January 1955

could find plus nails and ropes and a block and tackle. We then unloaded the mail.

We ended up with more than enough material and built a long platform around the nose of the aircraft, on which we erected an "A" frame lean-to over the propeller hub, and a long line going out to a Deadman secured in the ice. On this we secured our Block and Tackle, and before dark we had the aircraft skis well clear of the ice, with planks laid under them to support the aircraft until — after a night of freezing temperature — the aircraft could be lowered back unto its undercarriage again.

The area where we had broken through had been a large crack in the Bay ice about ten feet wide which had frozen over. With a light layer of snow it was impossible to see it, and unfortunately no one had bothered to mark it as unsafe.

The following day, March 1, was clear and cold and there was now at least eight inches of hard slush ice under the aircraft. We lowered the Otter onto the platform and pulled the aircraft clear of the area. On inspecting the aircraft it was

January 1955 Salvage operations, Otter CF-GCV at Black Tickle

found to be free of damage, and after heating up the engine we started up with no difficulty and taxied back to the inner bay where we secured the aircraft for the night, planning to fly back to Gander the next morning. I advised Gander of our progress and intentions.

The weather was not suitable for flight the next morning, however we utilized the time in returning all the material and gear to Mr. Earl's shed.

We departed Black Tickle in marginal weather on March 3 and, with another refuelling stop at Roddickton, landed at Gander in mid-afternoon.

A pleasant flight was flown on April 24 and 25 when I took delivery of another Republic Seabee, CF-DLS, purchased from Joe Folkins of Moncton N.B., and flew it via Sydney and Buchans to Gander. We felt this little amphibian could fill an operational requirement in between seasons in our fleet.

Another enjoyable flight was the delivery of a Fleet Canuck CF-DEN from Gander to Saint John N.B. This

Ready For National Flying Club Week

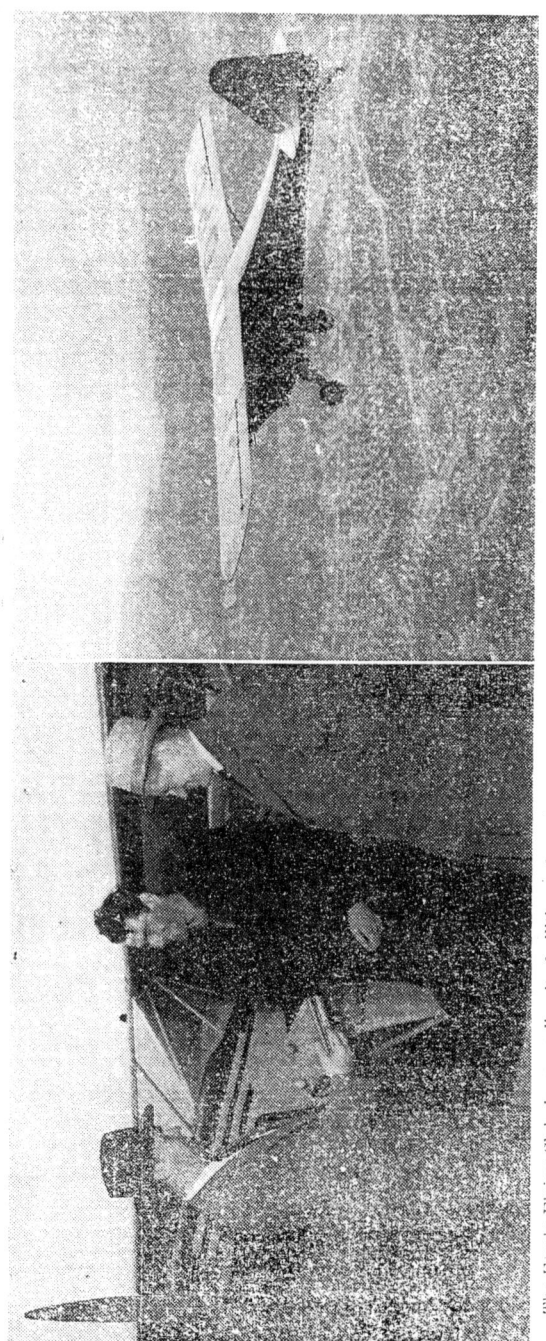

The Fundy Flying Club, in expanding its facilities and services to meet growing membership, this week purchased a reconditioned "Fleet Canuck" two-seater trainer aircraft—giving it a total of five aircraft. At top left is pictured the reconditioned airplane, shortly after its landing at the Saint John Airport. Handing over the airplane's log books to Hugh H. McElligott, president of Fundy Flying Club, is Marsh Jones (centre), of Eastern Provincial Airways. Mr. Jones flew the aircraft from Gander, Newfoundland, to Saint John. Standing at right is R. D. Bardsley, treasurer for the Fundy Flying Club. At top right is shown another of the club's fleet of aircraft, winging over Portland Place in Saint John. The photograph was snapped from a second aircraft, which accompanied the one pictured at right in a 30-minute warm-up flight over the city.

This photo is from the Saint John *Evening Times-Globe*, and reports on the delivery of the Fleet Canuck CF-DEN to the Fundy Flying Club

Fleet Canuk CF-DEN, bought from insurance company by Marsh Jones and Bill Harris. It was repaired and sold to the Saint John Flying Club in New Brunswick.

aircraft had been owned by the St. John's Flying Club and had been damaged in a landing accident. Bill Harris and I bought it from the insurance company and repaired it. It was subsequently bought by the Saint John Flying Club in Saint John, N.B. I departed Gander on May 18 with refuelling stops at Buchans, St. Andrews (on the highway where I refuelled from a five gallon can), Sydney, Moncton and on to Saint John. A long day — nine hours and fifty minutes — in a small single-engine aircraft on wheels.

During June 28 and 29 I flew our only Cessna 180 CF-HCJ to Toronto via Buchans, Havre St. Pierre (north shore), Bay Comeau, Malbaie and Lac-à-la-Tortue. It was sold to a aircraft broker to the credit of Wheeler Airlines as payment for their interest in our Canso CF-HFL.

I met Jim Lewington in Toronto where on June 30 we took delivery of Beaver CF-IHK and delivered it to Gander via Lac-à-la-Tortue, Knob Lake where we touched base with our crews on the mid-Canada operations (pilots Clibbery, Packer, Moore). Then on to Goose and Gander. This Beaver IHK had a custom interior and was assigned to the IGA contract in St. Anthony.

Summer operations kept all five Beavers, one Norseman QAA, the Seabee DLS busy with the Otter and Canso on the mid-Canada Line. Three of the Beavers were committed to

Lockheed CF-BXE

Government contracts, Department of Health (IGA), NALCO and Department of Mines and Resources, Tourism, (hunting and fishing) was particularly heavy between Gander and Walls Pond, Berry Hill Pond, Middle Ridge Pond, Little Gander Pond, Newton Pond, Berry Hill Pond and Gander First, Second and Third Pond fishing camps.

During the summer construction of airstrips at Frenchman's Cove on the Burin Peninsula and Deer Lake near Corner Brook opened up the possibilities of tying up these points with a passenger service to St. John's and Gander. With this in mind two Lockheed 10 aircraft, CF-BXE and CF-HTV were bought in late December with the intention of starting a service in the spring of 1956. These were all metal, twin-engine ten-passenger aircraft, with retractable undercarriage and a cruising speed of 150 knots.

The year ended with our revenues up by $150,000 over 1954 and outlook for 1956 was very optimistic.

Jim Macgillivary joined us as Office Manager and Accountant, replacing John Anstey who opened up his own business in Gander.

Chapter 11

Flight Operations 1956

This was a year of much activity wherein our Beaver fleet numbered ten, together two Lockheeds, the Canso, the Seabee, the Otter, a Bell Ranger Helicopter, and a leased DC-3 which brought our total fleet to eighteen. Four Beavers were purchased, CF-GCQ, CF-GQF, CF-JAT and CF-IVA and one wet-leased CF-GYN from Maritime Central Airways and flown by Myles Curry. The extra Beaver was required to fill commitments after the loss of Beaver CF-IHK

Beaver CF-IHK at St. Anthony
January 1956

CF-IVE
Clayton Hutchings, Doug Moore, Marsh Jones

on take-off from St. Anthony. The aircraft was a complete write-off with fortunately no injuries to pilot Don Ballantyne and his passengers. New pilots hired were Jim Roe, Clayton Hutchings, Geoff Henderson, Peter Crux, Harry Drover, Cyril Jones, Ian Massie and Gill Wass.

After a successful winter mail operation where the mail revenues exceeded those of the previous winter, tragedy struck on May 12 when our new Bell Helicopter CF-IVF hit a power line on take-off and crashed at the Smallwood farm (Russwood), killing the pilot Gill Wass and a passenger, and injuring two others. These were the first fatalities in our operations. The Helicopter was replaced by CF-IVE.

With the oncoming passenger service planned for the Lockheeds it was time to upgrade my qualifications by obtaining an Instrument Rating. I had qualified on the type after a checkout from Roy Cooper who was now the Chief Pilot, and had done a number of flights as Captain on various flights to Knob Lake, Seven Islands, ice patrols for AND Co etc. It was now necessary to get some formal instrument instruction

Flight Operations 1956

Seabee CF-DLS
Pilot Ian Massie

which was obtained at the "Advanced School of Link Training" in Montreal.

After completion of the course I received a formal checkout by Bob Graham of MCA on our Canso HFL which was ready to return to Gander after extensive modifications and repairs by Timmins Aviation in Montreal. Jim Lewington and I flew it back to Gander on March 3.

I finally received my Class 1 Instrument Rating from Jimmy Dale, an MOT inspector, on Lockheed BXE May 2, 1956.

Our scheduled Lockheed passenger service between St. John's, Frenchman's Cove, Gander and Deer Lake started on May 28. Roy Cooper and I captained these flights with Glen McClusky acting as first officer.

Jim Lewington and I picked up the two Beavers GCQ and GQF which we purchased from Rimouski Airlines on June 7 and flew them to Gander via Havre St. Pierre for refuelling. During the summer we moved our seaplane base from Gander Lake to Deadmans Pond. This required building new floating dockage, building a dam at the outlet to raise the water by two feet, and the construction of a small waiting room and maintenance shed to support the operation. This move proved to be extremely beneficial providing convenience for our passengers as well as increased operational reliability.

Our involvement on the DEW Line proceeded well with our arrangement with Trans Labrador Airlines in the wet-lease of two DC-3s, CF-BZN and ILZ, and the wet-lease of a Canso CF-HGE on the mid-Canada Line. While our mid-Canada Line contract was completed in late 1956, the lease of the two DC-3s on the DEW Line continued into 1957. Additional Beaver work required an aircraft based full time at North West River with the Department of Health/IGA and a summer requirement by Bowaters at Corner Brook.

Two significant flights stand out in my memory of 1956. The first involved Lockheed BXE on July 7.

Tom Antle of the Anglo Newfoundland Development Company at Grand Falls called me early on the evening of July 6, requesting an ice survey over the mouth and approaches to Exploits Bay the next morning, as early as daylight would permit. They had a ship due in Botwood for a load of paper and indications were that there was some ice around information of which was required to pass on to the captain. I promised Tom I would be airborne bright and early the next morning. I alerted maintenance to have Lockheed BXE serviced with two main tanks of fuel and ready for a 0700 departure.

The weather was favourable when I arrived at the hangar the next morning to find BXE ready to go. I did my flight planning and preflight check and started up, did my take-off check, received take-off clearance and proceeded to take off on runway twenty-seven at Gander. Up to then everything was normal but at first power reduction both engines lost all power. I was about one hundred feet above the runway with half the runway remaining and decided to try and land. The alternative was the water of Gander Lake which was directly ahead!

A lot of thoughts can go through your mind in a matter of seconds. I knew I was too low to try and re-start the engines so I dumped full flaps shut off the magneto switches and decided to land on the belly with the gear up. I lowered the nose to maintain gliding speed and descended very fast. Immediately before touching the runway I raised the flaps. After much scraping and banging the aircraft came to a stop about fifty feet from the end of the runway. All was quiet except the tower was frantically inquiring if I was ok. I advised them I had had a double engine failure, and that I was ok and to please advise EPA operations. Outside the aircraft there appeared to be no damage except for the two propellers which were curled backwards. With the undercarriage in the retracted position at least half the wheels are below the engine cowl (which protected the airplane on landing). Knowing the engines had failed due to apparent fuel starvation I went back into the cockpit and checked the fuel gauges and tanks selectors. The two main tanks were full and the two auxiliary tanks were empty. Both selectors were on the auxiliary tanks. I had taken off on dry tanks! After some thought it occurred to me that I had taken off on the full main tanks and it immediately became clear that having flown our other Lockheed CF-HTV for a number of hours in the previous week, and with her arrangement of selectors and tanks being quite different from BXE, I had selected the main tanks on BXE as if I were selecting the mains on HTV. The selector pointing to main tanks on HTV actually point to auxiliary on BXE. This is a perfect case for uniformity and standardization of similar types. However my face was red over that one!

The second flight was flown on December 8 to 11 in Beaver CF-EYQ on wheel/skis with mail for Cartwright and

Hopedale in Labrador. I had taken along another pilot, Geoff Henderson, who had been with us on the summer operation but was unfamiliar with the winter operation on wheel/skis. This would be a familiarization flight for him. As it was early in the winter season, landing conditions were not safe as yet in Newfoundland. It was therefore necessary to fly non-stop to Cartwright, where a landing was made well inside the harbour on an area marked out with tree tops. The landing was uneventful and we were airborne again in a few minutes with Geoff at the controls. Overhead Hopedale we could see the landing markers laid out in an area parallel to the main harbour area. The area looked rough with heavy snow drifts. We would have to land however, as we did not have sufficient fuel to return to Cartwright, or proceed to Goose Bay.

The approach was flown landing to the west into a 20 mph wind. Touch-on was smooth, followed by several severe bumps and, as the tail ski settled, a loud crack. The Beaver came to a stop and I looked at Geoff and said "We've got a damaged tail section!" Geoff shut down the engine and we left the aircraft to inspect the damage. Sure enough, the tail wheel/ski fork spindle was broken off at the yoke, and the metal skin on each side of the canted bulkhead was badly wrinkled. Since it was now dusk and necessary to stay all night, we secured the aircraft. I advised Gander operation of our problem and that I would contact them in the morning. We then waited for the mail courier who arrived in a little while. We loaded the mail and got on the komatik, and off we went to the village of Hopedale. At Hopedale we went to the Moravian Mission where we were kindly put up for the night.

The next morning it was blowing a blizzard when Eli Nitzman, our agent and mail courier, arrived. We set out for the aircraft so I could contact Gander by the aircraft radio. It took us about an hour to reach the Beaver. Gander operation advised that due to weather they could not send us a me-

Flight Operations 1956

chanic to help us, that the weather forecast was poor for the next day, and that maintenance wanted to know if I could clear away the tail wheel ski from the tail and take off and come directly to Gander and land in the snow alongside the runway. I told them I thought we could, so we left it at that. Actually there was little involved in clearing away the tail ski, just two clevis pins which held the ski cables. We also removed the tail cone as I felt we could further damage it on take-off and landing. When that was completed we went back to the village and returned to the aircraft with two forty-five gallon drums of gas and refuelled.

The weather on December 10 was still poor with some signs of clearing in late afternoon. Next morning the wind was 30 knots from the west and the visibility down in blowing snow, however it looked promising. Geoff and I dressed up, had breakfast, and tracked through the snow to Eli's where with little delay we were on the komatik and with six dogs tackled were swiftly off to the aircraft, arriving at around ten-thirty.

I called Gander and advised we would be taking off within the hour and inquired as to the weather. They advised it looked very good at the moment but a warm front was approaching the Gander area from the southwest and they expected deteriorating weather around late afternoon. This should give us about six or seven hours which should be enough time. They advised Goose was ok and if I felt I could not make Gander I should go on to Goose. As we had no maintenance support available in Goose, I decided on Gander.

It took us about an hour to heat and start the engine and clear the snow — which had a glaze of ice on it — from the wings and tail section. I decided I would fly the leg as I'd had more experience than Geoff, and he wasn't anxious to do the flight in any event. It was my intention to lift the tail as soon as possible and take off without taxiing. This was possible as we were headed just about directly into the strong westerly winds. After a prolonged warm up to ensure I had burned off the oil dilution, I did the take-off check, opened full take-off power, eased forward on the control column and with a few waggles on the rudder, the skis broke loose and we were moving. As we were fairly light, and with a strong headwind, we were airborne after a few bumps and set course for Gander 550 miles to the south via Cartwright, Mary's Harbour, Roddickton, Harbour Deep and Partridge Point to Gander. Airborne time 1150. With a ground speed of (hopefully) 100 mph we were estimating Gander at 1720, a little after dark. We passed overhead Cartwright at 1320 cruising at 3000 feet with the weather holding excellent. Mary's Harbour passed underneath at 1430. From now on there would not be any safe landing area this side of Buchans and Gander airports. Over Roddickton at 1530 an overcast had developed, lowering visibility to ten miles, but forecast to deteriorate further within a few hours.

Over Harbour Deep and starting to cross White Bay I noticed the first signs of clear icing. This was a source of concern, as apart from carburettor heat we were defenceless. I was very reluctant to descend to a warmer temperature as White Bay was open water and in the event of an engine problem it was desirable to have more gliding distance available. With the ice building up gradually, it was necessary to increase power to hold our altitude. Geoff was looking apprehensive and I'm sure I was as well. All sorts of alternative actions went through my mind. I knew if I got into real trouble I could possibly land on a woods road on the Baie Verte Peninsula. I certainly could not trust the ice on any of the lakes as the ice would not support the weight of the Beaver. However over and above these alternatives I was very anxious to get the aircraft to Gander where it could be repaired.

Halfway across White Bay I was using climb power with a little flap to maintain altitude and airspeed of 90 mph. The glaze of ice on the windshield was making it difficult to see so I was, in effect, flying by instruments. To add to everything it was now getting dusky. It was now 1615 and we were over Partridge Point at 2000 feet with the lights of Baie Verte showing a mile or so on our right. With any luck we could make Gander in an hour. I had gradually allowed the altitude to bleed off as we approached the east side of White Bay, hoping to get into a layer of warmer air. We were still picking up ice, however as we flew east I was expecting the temperature to rise and with lower land ahead I could afford to descend a little lower. It was now dark and we were over Green Bay.

Gander operations advised me the weather was still holding with no sign of icing. I advised them my estimated arrival was 1740 and that I was now running out of the icing at 1000 feet and asked them where was the best landing area. I was anxious to prevent further damage to our tailwheel-less airplane if possible. They advised me to land on runway fourteen and try and stop abeam our hangar taxiway. I had hoped to land on the side of the runway in deep snow to prevent further damage to the tail, but they felt with a compacted layer of snow on the asphalt, runway damage would be minimal. It was a welcome sight when the rotating beacon of Gander airport was visible. I contacted the tower about twenty miles out and received their clearance to land straight in on runway fourteen. With some relief we touched down at 1745, held the tail high for as long as possible and, with a scraping sound from the tail end, came to a stop abeam Hangar 22. Our maintenance staff were out with a dolly on castoring wheels, lifted the tail on it and towed the aircraft into the hangar.

1956 was the most active year in the company's history to that time. Revenues exceeded one million dollars for the first time, due mostly to our participation in the Defense construction mid-Canada and DEW Line projects, together with increases in mail and additional Beaver contracts with IGA at North West River, Bowater's summer contract and considerable flying for Terminal Construction on the Gap Filler Radar site at La Scie. Our total employment was now fifty-one, up from thirty-three in 1955 and thirty-one in 1954. New personnel joining us in 1956 were Bert Patey, heading our Flight Dispatch, together with Jim Davis and Lloyd Brown as Dispatchers.

Flight Operations — 1957

After a long cold winter with excellent ice conditions mail uplifted totalled 700,000 lbs. Our Otter GCV was extremely busy with the Dept of Defense production on supply to Hopedale and Cartwright Radar Station. Due to a heavy build-up of northern ice which blocked Bell Island, our Lockheeds were busy supplying it from St. John's airport. During a period of three weeks in March, Roy Cooper and I made over 180 flights there, landing on a good gravel strip — hastily prepared for the operation — on Neary's farm. Our Health contract for Beaver at St. Anthony and North West River continued. Our activities were less however in the DEW and mid-Canada Line projects as construction was completed and re-supply went to other airline companies.

Seal spotting for Bowring Brothers and ice spotting for the AND Co at Botwood was carried out with the Canso and Lockheed 10. Our passenger service between St. John's, Frenchmans Cove, Deer Lake and Gander was very disappointing, due mainly to lack of ground and navigational facilities, which caused inconvenience to passengers and irregularity of flights. Sydney was added to the service of St. Pierre and the leg Sydney/St. Pierre/Sydney showed much promise.

New pilots added to the operations were: Austin Garrett, Ron "Teet" Anonsen and co-pilots Lloyd Batten and Ron Smith.

Canso CF-HFL crashed after double engine failure, October 5, 1957 seventy-five miles northwest of Goose Airport

The summer operation showed increased activities over the previous summer. The Lockheeds were busy on the passenger service, four of our Beavers were on full time contracts and the additional flying with Bell Telephone using the Canso HFL between Goose Bay and Sona Lake (about 150 miles northwest of Goose) and increased construction on the Gap Filler sites — particularly La Scie — all added to a busy summer.

The operation to Sona Lake came to an abrupt halt on the evening of October 5 when we received a radio call from Captain Rivard telling us they'd had a double engine failure in the Canso and had crashed about seventy-five miles northwest of Goose, and that no injuries were sustained. However the aircraft was badly damaged. I advised him that a Beaver from Goose would pick them up first thing in the morning and that I would arrive at Goose later in the day.

Our insurance company and Ministry of Transport at Moncton were advised of the accident. Fred Deveau, the insurance adjuster, would arrive in Gander the following morning for transportation to Goose Bay, and MOT required an accident report when available.

Co-pilot Ron Smith   Captain Ben Rivard

Fred Deveau, Bill Harris and I left in Lockheed 10 CF-BXE immediately after Fred arrived from Montreal on T.C.A. the next morning.

After arriving at Goose we interviewed the Canso crew, Rivard, Smith and Jack Furey, who had arrived shortly before us from the accident site in a Beaver flown by Clayton Hutchings. The crew were completely baffled as to the cause of the double engine failure. I decided to proceed to the accident site in Beaver FHS and see if we could determine anything.

We found the wreck with no difficulty just inside from the shoreline of the lake which they had almost made on their forced landing the night before. The aircraft was a total write-off. Bill Harris and Fred Deveau, both aircraft engineers, set out immediately checking fuel, oil and hydraulic lines, and soon discovered the cause of the accident which was the actuation of the emergency fuel, oil shutoff switches located on the instrument panel opposite the co-pilot position. With these switches closed, all fuel, oil and hydraulic fluid were immediately shutoff to the engines, causing their failure.

Canso being airlifted by RCAF Chinook Helicopter

Canso on ramp at Goose Airport

We flew back to Goose and after further questioning of the crew, Smith, the co-pilot remembered running his fingers idly over the switches as he reached to turn on the instrument lights. Captain Rivard having no knowledge of the action was unable to recover or even take any recovering action, but had to land on as suitable terrain as possible. The lake mentioned earlier was almost reached, however the starboard wing struck some high trees that bordered the lake and swung the aircraft around in a 180° ground loop, causing severe damage to the structure.

The aircraft lay in that position for twenty-nine years until it was airlifted out in one piece — minus engine and undercarriage gear — by a large RCAF Chinook Helicopter to Goose on October 24, 1986, where it was subsequently dismantled and shipped by boat to Halifax to the Atlantic Aviation Museum which intends to set it up as a static display.

During November, while attending a convention in Quebec City, I ran into Vic Emery of Timmins Aviation who was demonstrating a Piaggo Royal Gull amphibian. I flew the

Royal Gull
CF-ILU

aircraft and, apart from some quirks on landing, it seemed like a good little machine to fit a slot in our fleet with its amphibian qualities and twin-engine capability.

We bought the aircraft and after its arrival in Gander on November 21 I decided to give it its initial flight to Nain, Labrador, with a load of mail. It was very late in the year for a water operation that far north, however Nain confirmed they had open water, so we gave it a go.

The post office delivered 800 lbs of mail to us that evening which we stowed in the main cabin behind the pilot seat and the large hull compartment behind the main cabin. An early start was necessary the next morning, as I would have to refuel at Goose on the way north and hopefully get back to Goose to overnight.

The weather looked excellent the next morning with a departure one hour before dawn. The aircraft was a real pleasure to fly and, with its two Lycoming engines mounted as pushers on its high gull wing, the noise level was quite low.

Due to a strong northwest wind the flight to Goose took three hours and thirty-five minutes, giving me a ground speed of 115 mph. My cruising airspeed was 145 mph. After landing at Goose I was met by our people who refuelled me and I was off again for the two hour flight to Nain.

As I flew north it was obvious that winter was here, with all the lakes frozen solid and the ground white with snow between the sparse spruce trees. Old familiar landmarks appeared one after another, Nipisish Lake, Seal Lake off to the west, the Kaipokok River flowing out past Postville, the Adlatuk River flowing into the Hopedale area, the Hunt River and Flowers River inside Davis Inlet then over Voisey Bay and into Nain. They had open water in the bay. However the wind was brisk from the northwest and vapour blowing in long streaks told me that the conditions were ripe for freezing spray. I circled several times and finally saw a boat put out from the long main wharf. I touched down in the relatively quiet water near the wharf as the wind was off shore. I taxied to the lee of the wharf, shutdown the engines and, with my towing line in hand, I opened the windshield door and threw up my line to a man on the wharf. With the boat alongside, we immediately transferred the mail to it, they signed my mail manifest and for the first time I really took a look at the airplane. It was literally covered with ice! As every splash of water hit the airplane it froze instantly. There were actually icicles hanging from the wing. What a situation to be in! I knew I couldn't possibly stay overnight and yet I doubted the aircraft could get airborne and fly safely with that much ice on it.

I decided to try a take-off. I let go the mooring line, let the aircraft drift back, then started the right engine and turned out towards the bay. I started the left engine and taxied down wind for half a mile. The bay water was getting very rough and I knew I should not go out any further so I let the airplane weathercock into the wind and did my take-off check leaving about half flap down. I took another look right and left at the icicles hanging from the bottom of the wings and thought if I got airborne and the aircraft feels too heavy I'd land immediately. I opened both throttles full and the reaction was encouraging as the aircraft jumped on the step and started to accelerate rapidly. At 60 mph she felt fine, however keeping the ice in mind I held her on a little longer then eased clear of the water. I could hardly see through the windshield because.of ice! I held full power on until I was sure of a positive rate of climb and when clear of the hills turned and set course for Goose.

The flight south to Goose took one hour and forty minutes, and during that time most of the ice eroded to the point where I was relatively free of ice when I landed. I stayed overnight at Goose and returned to Gander the next morning in a flying time of two hours and forty minutes.

The following day I checked out Roy Cooper, Benny Rivard and Gunner Laurell on the Gull.

After his checkout, Benny Rivard refused to fly it, considering it dangerous on water landings.

We subsequently received a modification from the factory in Italy adding seventeen inches to the step, making it quite docile on water landing. This was due to the centre of gravity which was now forward of the step.

To sum up, 1957 was discouraging, with expenses up and revenue flight hours down, caused mainly by a decrease in defense projects and extremely poor weather conditions in the latter half of the year.

Both Lockheed 10s and Beaver FHS were sold in December and plans were made to lease a DC-3 to replace the Lockheeds as well as a Canso to replace HFL which had been lost in Labrador in October.

DC-3
CF-JNR

Chapter 13

Flight Operations 1958

After an extremely mild winter when most of the Notre Dame and Bonavista North mail was delivered by helicopter and boat, some financial relief was obtained with an increase in bulk transportation to La Scie and St. Anthony for the USAF. In addition to this our Otter CF-GCV, flown by Jim Roe, was based in Frobisher for supply of bulk and passenger traffic to Resolution Island, located on the extreme southeast tip of Baffin Island at 62° north latitude. This aircraft experienced an engine failure in October and was fortunate to land on a small ice covered lake on the Lower Savage Islands near southeast Baffin Island, but

Canso CF-CRP
on ramp at Ivigtut, Greenland
October 1958

broke through the thin ice after landing. Pilot Roe and his three passengers were fortunate to escape injury and were later picked up by an American Coastguard ship. The aircraft was a complete write-off. It was replaced by a brand new Otter CF-LEA in mid-November. In the meantime the operation was continued with Beaver CF-GQU flown by Gunnar Laurell and crewman Gerry Finn.

Our leased Canso CF-CRP arrived May 8 and was kept reasonably busy on defense work to La Scie and St. Anthony together with ice patrols, until it was assigned a lucrative contract by the Danish Greenland Trade Department to carry out a number of ice survey flights from Mesters Vig in northeast Greenland. This requirement was to pass ice information to ships coming into Mesters Vig to load copper ore.

At the end of this operation the Canso proceeded to Sondrestrom "Bluie West eight" on the west side of Greenland to fly passengers from there to coastal points on the southwest coast. The crew on this successful operation — which produced 300 hours of revenue flying — was Captain Ben Rivard, Co-Pilot Ray Taylor and Flight Engineer Jack Furey.

Our leased DC-3 CF-JNR was picked up at Mont Jolie on June 2 by Roy Cooper who since 1956 was our Chief Pilot. I accompanied him and acted as Co-Pilot for the flight. I flew a number of flights with Roy during the next two weeks and received my type endorsement on June 16. This aircraft was used extensively during the summer months between Gander and St. John's to St. Pierre and return St. Pierre and Sydney. With the loss of Otter GCV on the Resolution Island contract in October, the decision was made to purchase a new Otter from DeHavilland. This aircraft, CF-LEA, was ready for delivery on November 5, at which time I test flew it in Toronto and accepted it on behalf of EPA. I departed Toronto on November 6 with Clayton Hodge as my crewman. We stopped at Montreal overnight and, with an early start the

Flight Operations 1958

Otter CF-LEA
at Fort Chimo
November 8, 1958

following morning, arrived Knob Lake — with a refuelling stop at Seven Islands — after seven hours of flying. This was as far north on this route as I had ever flown and I was eagerly looking forward to it.

The weather looked poor in the Frobisher and Hudson Straits the next morning. However it looked reasonable as far as Fort Chimo, Ungava Bay. Flying north that morning it was obvious that winter had set in as everything was sparkling white with snow. All the lakes were frozen solid but the rivers were still open. This was reassuring as our aircraft was equipped with wheel/skis making every lake a potential landing area. After nearly three hours of flying we landed on the paved runway at Fort Chimo and parked near a Nordair Beaver. Clayton arranged for refuelling from Nordair at $2.60 a gallon which was steep in those days. Fortunately we didn't need too much. We were accommodated that night in the Nordair bunkhouse and treated very well.

Fort Chimo airport was part of the wartime Crystal Route, and was known as Crystal 1, Frobisher as Crystal 2 and Cape Dyer as Crystal 3. Fort Chimo was now primarily a support airport for traffic to and from Frobisher and the DEW Line Defense chain.

Weather reports north were favourable the next morning so, after a hearty breakfast in the mess hall, we were airborne and flying up the west shoreline of Ungava Bay, over Cape Hopes Advance then over the Hudson Straits which was open and looking very cold and inhospitable. The south coastline of Baffin Island was visible in the distance and it too looked bleak and formidable. After a one hour crossing we were over Baffin Island and in radio contact with the tower in Frobisher. After receiving landing clearance, we touched down — four hours and thirty minutes from Fort Chimo.

That evening we agreed that Gunner and Clayton would fly the Otter to Resolution and Gerry Finn (Gunner's crewman) and I would take Beaver GQU on to Resolution and from there proceed south to Gander.

The next morning, November 10, we were airborne following the Otter to Resolution Island situated off the southeast tip of Baffin Island. The USAF had a radio station there and a small airstrip. EPA's contract was to supply mail and bulk goods as well as the rotation of personnel from Frobisher to there. The airstrip was 1200 feet long and 75 feet wide with a gravel surface and placed on top of the Island at 500 feet above sea level. The east end had a shear drop of 500 feet into the sea and the west end dropped into a deep gorge.

Gunner had already landed so I circled, giving the airstrip a good inspection before setting up an approach to the west. The wind was down the runway at about 20 mph. I selected landing flap and kept the speed a little high expecting a downdraft near the threshold. It wasn't too bad however, and I touched on about 400 feet in, and taxied to the

Flight Operations 1958

Otter CF-LEA and Beaver CF-GQU
at Resolution
November 10, 1958

west end where a small parking apron was cleared of snow. The USAF refuelled our Beaver and we were airborne within a half hour heading south with the intention of making Saglek radar station on the Labrador coast for the night. We were forty-five minutes south approaching Cape Chidley when Resolution called us advising that Saglek weather was down in an obscured snow condition with nil visibility. As this was no place to fool around in that kind of weather we advised Resolution we would be returning for the night. We landed there after one hour and thirty minutes flying and put the aircraft away for the night. In our absence the Otter had returned to Frobisher.

We spent a very enjoyable evening as guests of the USAF The food and accommodation were excellent. There was also a good movie.

Next morning with the weather fine and clear we got away after an early breakfast, and in clear skies and light winds the Button Islands, then Cape Chidley, Labrador, soon passed, followed by the rugged Torngat mountains. The radar station Dome at Saglek was now visible in the distance. I had radio contact now with Saglek and they advised me that the weather at the southern station of Hopedale and Goose was giving low visibility in snow. I gave them my ETA[1] for Saglek and inquired as to accommodation for the night. They advised no problem. I requested fuel and they advised the fuel and transportation would be laid on.

We landed on their paved snow-cleared runway after a three hour flight from Resolution Island.[2]

With the aircraft securely tied down and refuelled we drove up the hill 2000 feet above sea level to the radar station, where we were to spend the next three days sitting out a blinding blizzard. During the first morning I received a message from Gander to proceed to Indian House Lake and pick up a seriously ill weather observer and fly him to Goose. By return message I requested that the weather station at Indian House flag the landing area to confirm sufficient ice for the landing.

The morning of November 14 was crisp and clear. The radar station was beautiful to look at with the sculptured main pattern created by the wind action and tons of snow around the interconnecting walkways between the various buildings. However on the winding road down to the airstrip it was almost bare. The aircraft was in good shape but there was a lot of snow on the runway which had not been ploughed as yet. This didn't bother us as I would lower the skis and take off on the snow.

---

1 Estimated time of arrival.
2 It was here that a USAF B-26 medium bomber force-landed on December 10, 1942 where, after surviving for nearly two months, all crew members perished. Remains of the aircraft were still visible at this time.

We started up with no problem and after engine warm-up extended the skis and with a short burst of power we were taxiing out for take-off. As we were very light, we were airborne after a short run and climbing to the southwest to Indian House Lake 175 miles inland, inside the Quebec border. In an hour and forty-five minutes we were over Indian House Lake weather station and saw a line of small tree tops imbedded in the snow-covered ice surface, just off from the station. I landed and shut down close to the building.

The operator who greeted me was anxious to get his co-worker to hospital as soon as possible so we did not delay. They carried him to the Beaver on a stretcher and were relieved when they saw I had a crewman (Gerry Finn) with me who would act as an attendant for the patient. We started up and took off, turned to a southeasterly heading and within two and a half hours were landing at Goose where the waiting ambulance conveyed our patient to hospital. Once again weather delayed us and it was the morning of November 16 we finally made good our last leg to Gander, where we arrived after a three and a half hour flight.

1958 ended on a good note as, unlike the previous year, it looked as though we would have excellent winter weather with increased mail and revenues.

Our aircraft fleet at the end of 1958 consisted of: One DC-3 CF-JNR — leased; one Canso CF-CRP — leased; eight Beavers (CF-IVA, EYQ, EYW, GQU, JAT, GQF, GCQ, GBD); one Royal Gull, CF-ILU; one Bell Ranger, CF-IVE.

New pilots added to operations were Harry Drover, Hubert Rodway and Ray Taylor.

Chapter 14

Flight Operations 1959

As predicted this turned out to be a busy year producing gross revenues of $1,139,320.00 with nearly 10,000 hours logged. Our winter mail season delivered nearly 800,000 lbs of mail which, together with provincial government and USAF contracts, gave us a good financial base for a change. A new Otter CF-PMQ on amphibian floats was purchased from Timmins Aviation for $90,000. Both the Canso CF-CRP and DC-3 CF-JNR previously leased were purchased from Trans-Labrador Airlines and United Helicopters with its principle asset of one Sikorski S-55 Helicopter was purchased for $120,000. Our St. Pierre operations were reduced to occasional charters due to renewed competition from Maritime Central Airways. Our contract with the USAF at Frobisher/Resolution for one Otter terminated on June 30. Canso CF-CRP, under the command of Captain Rivard, once again proceeded to Greenland where it carried out a passenger service between Sondrestrom and a number of points on the southwest coast. It returned to Gander late in October after a very successful operation, and an indication from the Danish Government that it would be interested in a yearly operation involving two Otters and one Canso.

During the winter and continuing on into the summer a number of cable patrols were carried out for Eastern Telephone and Telegraph Company at Sydney. This kept our DC-3 JNR busy together with a number of profitable charters from St. John's and Stephenville with workers going to the newly opened Iron Ore operation at Carol Lake in Labrador, later to become Wabush.

While our exposure to accident damage was normally high due to the majority of take-offs and landings being from unprepared surfaces, especially with our bush type aircraft, we had an unfortunate accident at Musgrave Harbour in July when Beaver CF-GQU, piloted by Harry Drover, was written-off during a rough water landing. Fortunately no one was injured. Insurance was one of our highest cost items because of our exposure to accident damage. Our premium rates on the small bush aircraft was upwards of 20%[1]

In browsing through my log book for 1959, I found my activities involved a variety of aircraft including Otters, Beavers, Cansos, Royal Gull, DC-3 and a check out on a Grumman Goose CF-JDH by John Bogie of Laurentide Aviation from Ottawa. The Canso and DC-3 flights consisted of cable patrols, ice patrols, general charters and mail flights.

One very interesting series of flights took place in southwest Greenland October 17 – 20, when after a meeting in Sondrestrom with the Danish Greenland Trade officials and their Civil Aviation Authorities, it was emphasized that they would require an Operations Manual from us. The manual would cover the Greenland operations together with landing charts of all the places we would operate into, including Instrument Cloud Breaking Procedures and Enroute VFR and IFR route charts. This was a big undertaking as apart from topographical maps of the area nothing else could be provided by the Danes. It was therefore our responsibility to provide them! Obviously I had a job on my hands! As Director of Flight Operations I was responsible for our operation and the first thing was to familiarize myself with the area.

---

1 20% of the replacement cost of the aircraft. Bush aircraft were prone to damage due to landing on unprepared surfaces such as rough ice, snowdrifts, rough water, etc.

The following morning we departed Sondrestrom in Canso CF-CRP and made landings at Holsteinborg, Egedesminde, Sukertoppen, Godthab and returned to Sondrestrom. Photos and sketches of landing areas were made at each point as well as flying a simulated cloud breaking procedure at each place. Flights in between were made at minimum altitude. The same routine was carried out the following day to Frderikshaab, Ivigtut, Julianahaab, Narsassuak, Godthab and back to Sondrestrom. This involved fifteen hours of flying and provided me with enough information to get the manual and series of charts on the drawing board.

I returned to Goose the following day by a MATS[2] Douglas C-124.

On November 20 the new dirt strip near St. Anthony was ready. It was located at the southwest corner of Pistolet Bay about eighteen miles from St. Anthony. I made the first landing there with Beaver CF-GQF on wheel/skis and left the aircraft there for the Grenfell operation and returned with their Beaver CF-JAT on floats to Gander for its change-over to wheel skis.

The year ended with my presence being required to fly forty odd hours of DC-3 time which pleased me no end. It was without doubt one of my favourite aircraft.

Aircraft in operation at the end of 1959 were: One DC-3, CF-JNR; one Canso, CF-CRP; two Otters, CF-LEA and CF-PMQ; seven Beavers (CF-IVA, EYQ, EYW, JAT, GQF, GCQ, GBD); one Royal Gull, CF-ILU; one Bell Ranger, CF-IVE; one Sikorsky S-55, CF-HGU.

Number of personnel: 58.

---

2 Military Air Transport Service

Chapter 15

1960

This year exceeded all other years, including 1959, with gross revenues of $1,615,214.00. Mail revenues were down slightly from 1959 at $302,753.00. Passenger revenues were $46,332.00. Bulk transportation $1,050,685.00, including Greenland, which produced $270,000.00. Employees jumped to sixty-seven from fifty-eight in 1959. Insurance rates were 15 to 21% on various types. We realized a net income before taxes of $165,931.00

ACTIVITIES:
During the year purchase of three Otters was required to meet the demands of the Department of Health for one Otter CF-MIT to replace the St. Anthony Beaver, which was moved to Northwest River for the Department of Health. The Greenland operation required the purchase of Otter CF-MEX. There was a USAF requirement for one Otter CF-EYO, based in St. Anthony for supply to their radar stations. The provincial Department of Mines and Resources utilized one Beaver together with one each to Bowaters, AND Co, and the Federal Government Geological survey in the Shapio Lake area of Labrador. The Iron Ore development at Wabush (then called Carol Lake), together with the Twin Falls Hydro development kept our DC-3 busy.

Additional activity involved the cable patrols for the Eastern Telephone and Telegraph Company.

Canso CF-CRP refueling Otter CF-LEA at Fort Chimo
on the way to Greenland

Our first involvement with the phase-out of Fort Pepperell took place when we obtained a contract for furniture movement to Stephenville and Goose Bay using a Curtis C-46, CF-IQJ, leased from World Wide Aviation and flown by Captain Ellie Yeomans. Our involvement in the St. Pierre operation was disappointing once again, due to competition from Maritime Central Airways.

Our most interesting operation involved the requirement for two Otters and one Canso to carry out internal flying operations in southwest Greenland. The three aircraft: Otter CF-LEA flown by Jack Kielley, Otter CF-MEX flown by Ian Massie and Canso CF-CRP flown by Ben Rivard and Paul Bjerg — together with supporting maintenance crews and spares — departed Gander April 26 with refuelling stops at Goose, Knob Lake, Fort Chimo, Frobisher, Cape Dyer, and arrived Sondrestrom Greenland the following day. All aircraft were amphibious, allowing them to operate from the runway at Sondrestrom, and on water at the coastal points.

Otters on the ramp at Godthab, Greenland

I accompanied the aircraft to set up the operation and do additional survey work to complete the operation manual, together with the landing and cloud breaking charts to support the operation and to satisfy the Danish Civil Authorities.

During the following four weeks all operational requirements were met and approved by the Danish CAA, and a very efficient and safe operation was set up with continuous flight watch and thirty minutes "normal operation" broadcast by all aircraft and monitored by the CAA, together with waterborne tenders[1] at all landing points. Arrangements had also been made for the provision of a parking area and ramp to be built at Godthab to accommodate the two amphibious Otter aircraft, to enable them to be washed down and maintained out of the salt water environment

Our crew were accommodated in the SAS Hotel in Sondrestrom and the Greenland Trade Hotel in Godthab.

---

1 Floating installation to provide fuel and servicing.

Our Chief Pilot Roy Cooper relieved me at the end of May, and for the rest of the year we alternated shifts.

On my return from Greenland I did a series of flights with Captain Yeomans in the Curtis C-46 CF-IQJ. I had had a checkout on type on April 9. This aircraft was the largest I'd flown to date, and to me even the Canso and the DC-3 were dwarfed by it. With its powerful Pratt and Whitney R-2800 engines it had twice the DC-3 payload and was about 25 knots faster. I was fascinated by the high, comfortable cockpit compartment.

On June 16 we did a furniture haul from Stephenville to Moncton, and the following day flew from Gander to Goose Bay with furniture as well. Both flights were for the USAF. On this second flight Ellie acted as co-pilot and I occupied the captain seat. It was a thoroughly enjoyable experience.

There were a few other flights of interest during the year.

On March 15, with DC-3 CF-JNR equipped with wheel skis, I made a mail delivery from Gander to Labrador: to Makkovik, Postville, Hopedale, Davis Inlet and Nain, then into Goose for refuelling and home to Gander. Ben Rivard was my co-pilot, and the flight was carried out in excellent conditions, with a foot of snow on the bay ice.

The action of the skis was automatically trimmed by an airfoil wing on the ski tail, and cables limited their travel. The actuation was hydraulic via a selector. The skis tucked up against the engine nacelles[2] in the retracted position. They did however provide some drag with the resultant airspeed 10 – 12 knots below normal.

On April 21 I took delivery of a new Otter from DeHavilland in Toronto. The aircraft was on amphibious floats and was destined to Greenland. A single refuelling stop was made

---

2 The housing which covers the engines.

Otter CF-MIT on arrival at Gander from Toronto

at Moncton, then on to Gander, for a total flying time of eleven hours.

Another new Otter was bought, and my family accompanied me on the delivery flight from Toronto, on July 6. CF-MIT was destined to become the I.G.A. flag ship based in St. Anthony under the direction of Dr. Gordon Thomas.

Aircraft leaving Hanger 20 for new quarters in Hanger 22, Gander

This trip was a real experience for my two kids. Rick, my son, was nine and Lesley, my daughter was seven.

Our routing was down the north shore of the St. Lawrence with stops at Lac-à-la-Tortue and overnight at Seven Islands, then non-stop the following day to Gander. Flying time was eleven hours and five minutes.

Of great significance was our movement from Hangar 20 to Hanger 22 at Gander. This was possible due to the opening of the new International Passenger Terminal at Gander. The new quarters were extensively renovated to accommodate our growing operation.

Four new pilots joined the company: Two Danes, Paul Bjerg and Eric Brorup, also Len Byl and Walter Brown.

Chapter 16

Bushline to Airline 1961

This was a year of expansion, with the inauguration in May of our new regular Class II passenger service between St. John's, Gander and Deer Lake and a Class II regular passenger service between St. John's, Gander, Deer Lake, Twin Falls and Wabush. This additional operation required the purchase of two DC-3s — CF-QBM and CF-CRW — both aircraft in a twenty-four seat configuration. Additional crews were hired which for the first time included Flight Attendants. They were Lynn Burke, Heidi Victor, Jane Keeping and Francis Cook, all in new gray/blue EPA

DC-3s CF-QBM and CF-CEW on ramp at Gander, carrying their new EPA colours

uniforms, and the aircraft in white/red/black trim livery with the large black EPA on its tail.

Our activities increased in other fields, such as the St. Lawrence Gulf ice reconnaissance, which at times involved two DC-3s and a Cessna 310 on charter from Laurentide Aviation.

The cable patrol for Eastern Telephone and Telegraph was increased to two to three patrols per week, with the customer requiring a DC-3 equipped with weather radar, Decca Navigator and Loran. This equipment was installed in DC-3 CF-ILW purchased in June from Eastern Canada Stevedoring. The USAF continued to utilize our Otter to support their radar station at St. Anthony. A serious outbreak of forest fires in Newfoundland kept our small aircraft fleet and Bell Helicopter extremely busy. The provincial Wildlife and Forestry and the Geological Survey of Canada, together with the Department of Health at St. Anthony and North West River, all utilized Otters and Beavers.

The winter mail service continued at a normal pace with increased rates for a two-year contract, resulting in increased revenues.

C-46s CF-NAD and CF-NAE

In early February controlling interest was bought in Wellon Flying Service at South Brook, which owned two Cessna 180 aircraft: CF-HDK, CF-LFH.

To support the other increased activities two DC-3s — CF-CRW, CF-QBM — were purchased for scheduled operation. One DC-3, CF-ILW, for charters and AT&T cable patrols. A Canso CF-IHA was added to the Greenland operation and Canso IIW to the Newfoundland operation for charters on a short-term lease basis. DC-3 CF-ILZ replaced DC-3 CF-JNR which was written-off in a take-off accident in St. Pierre on April 4. A C-46 CF-IQQ was leased for scheduled operation into Labrador.

Two fifty-seat C-46 aircraft, CF-NAD and CF-NAE, were purchased from Nordair in December to supplement the increased passenger traffic to Labrador.

In addition to the Wellons Flying Service purchase, four new Cessna 185s — CF-NBL, NBN, NBM and NNR — were added.

The year brought with it a rash of accidents which put a damper to all our achievements.

DC-3 CF-JNR, flown by Capt Rivard, was written off in a runway accident in St. Pierre on April 4. Fortunately there were no injuries. Cessna 180 CF-HDK had an engine failure in August and crashed near Notre Dame Junction. It was a total write-off. Fortunately again the pilot, Hubert Rodway, was not injured. Otter CF-MEX was written-off in our Greenland operation on August 29, due to in-flight fire and subsequent forced landing. The loss of this aircraft resulted in the tragic death of pilot James Roe. His gallantry and professional skill saved the lives of his four passengers and crewman Harris Robinson. Cessna 185 CF-NBN was written off in a landing accident near Rainey Lake west of Buchans in September, and again fortunately there were no injuries to pilot Dave Lang.

New pilots hired in 1961 were: Ellie Yeomans, Cliff

Fielding, Bent Nielson, Boyd Hefford, Maurice Charron, Syd Greeley, Vince Keyes, Hal Lowe, Lief Jorgensen and Peter Chalmers.

Total revenue for the year was $2,181,414.00 with 15,176 revenue hours and 1,651,622 revenue miles flown.

Aircraft fleet at the end of the Year: Two C-46s, CF-NAD, CF-NAE; three DC-3s, CF-QBM, CF-CRW, CF-ILW; two Cansos, CF-CRP, CF-IHA; (C-46 CF-IQQ, DC-3 CF-ILZ and Canso CF-IIW had been on short term lease); four Otters, CF-LEA, CF-PMQ, CF-EYO, CF-MIT; seven Beavers, CF-GBD, CF-EYQ, CF-EYW, CF-IVA, CF-GQF, CF-GCQ, CF-JAT; one Royal Gull, CF-ILU; three helicopters — Bell 47J CF-IVE, Sikorsky S-55 CF-GHV, Sikorsky S-55 CF-HGU. Wellons Flying Service: One Cessna 180 CF-LFH; three Cessna 185s, CF-NBL, CF-NBM, CF-NNR.

During the year our total employees increased to 123.

In looking over the year in my personal Logbook I find I'd flown a little over 500 hours in many varied aircraft over many varied flights. Included were four inspection trips to Greenland covering five weeks.

My first and second trips to Greenland, both of which involved inspection flights on Otter wheel/ski aircraft, were to many points never landed on before by aircraft. Each arrival attracted hundreds of curious onlookers, many of whom had not seen an aircraft before. Landings were carried out on skiis using frozen harbours or nearby ponds or water reservoirs. In Jacobshavn and Godhaab we used a nearby frozen snow-covered marsh.

This winter service did not use the Canso as it had been withdrawn for the winter months. However we were to re-assess our thinking on this, as it was not feasible to operate the wheel/ski aircraft south of Sondrestrom due lack of ice and suitable landing areas. The decision was made, with the Danish approval, to use a Canso on water operation the following winter in the southern points south of Sondrestrom.

My third trip to Greenland was made on May 31 when I picked up a newly purchased Canso CF-IHA at St. John, Quebec and with Cliff Fielding as my co-pilot flew it to Sondrestrom in twelve hours and forty minutes to start off the summer schedule.

During the next ten days we covered all southern points as far south as Narsassuak (old Bluie West 1).

During these flights I gave Cliff Fielding his captain checkout which left me free to do an Otter trip with CF-LEA, on amphibious floats to Umanak and Upernavik well up the west coast. Upernavik is actually at 73° north latitude. It was the most northern point I had ever flown, being some 350 miles north of Sondrestrom. This coast was very rugged with many small glaciers and many coastal mountain peaks over 1000 feet. Our route took us north of Sondrestrom over Christianshaab, the huge glacier at Jacobshavn, up the east side of Disko Bay, over the Nugssuag peninsula with our first landing at Umanak a small island with a 1000 foot mountain straight up from the sea. I had landed here on ice on March 17 with CF-MEX on wheel/skis.

We tied up to a moored boat in the small harbour and had a very enjoyable lunch with the local Greenland Trade Manager. We were airborne again after a short business session and on our way to Upernavik, 150 miles north.

Our weather was absolutely perfect which allowed us to cruise at 5000 feet, giving an excellent panoramic view of the coast ahead and the inland ice cap which rose to 10,000 feet. Our destination was in sight well over thirty miles away. I was concerned with the amount of floating ice in the various bays and inlets. However, at Upernavik its sheltered harbour was free of ice, and allowed us ample room for our type of aircraft.

While the Danish officials carried out their business, Morris Power, my crewman, arranged for a couple of drums

Start of trip to northern Greenland with Danish C.A.A. officials, 1961

Umanak, Greenland
Winter 1961

Crowds of onlookers at Godhavn, Greenland

Canso CF-CRP taxiing before takeoff at Godthab, Greenland

of aviation gas to be pumped into LEA's tanks. We then took a short walk around the village and like all Greenland villages the houses were very clean and colourful with typical nordic architecture, utilizing much decorative façade and trim. The majority of the population were Greenlanders (Inuit) with a small percentage of Danes. After a short visit my passengers were ready to return to Sondrestrom where we landed after a non-stop flight of three hours and twenty-five minutes.

Our routing on the return flight took us directly over Qutligssat on the north coast of Disko Island.

I left Sondrestrom on June 16 with Otter CF-LEA and with Morris Power as my crewman and in sixteen hours overall and fourteen hours and ten minutes flying time arrived Gander with refuelling stops at Frobisher and Goose. The last three hours were at night. However we had very good visual conditions all the way.

I returned this Otter to Sondrestrom on September 21 via Goose, Saglek and Frobisher to replace Otter CF-MEX which was destroyed by fire on August 29.

The following day after arrival Sondrestrom I flew in LEA to a lake just a few miles north (where CF-MEX had burnt) and viewed the wreck. I returned to Gander on September 27 with Canso CF-CRP non-stop in eight hours and forty minutes hours with Paul Bjerg as my co-pilot.

For the balance of the year I flew various aircraft on different types of flights from the Cessna 185 to the Curtis C-46 CF-IQQ, which covered our scheduled operation with landing at Deer Lake, Twin Falls, Wabush, Twin Falls, Deer Lake, St. John's and Gander. CF-IQQ was released off contract shortly after.

A highlight that fall was a flight from Stephenville to Deer Lake, and Deer Lake to Gander in DC-3 CF-ILW with Prime Minister Diefenbaker as our honoured guest. Vince Keyes was my first officer.

Chapter 17

Flight Operations 1962

As experienced in recent years our volume of business exceeded previous years with a gross revenue of $2,500,000. Scheduled services across the island and Labrador increased significantly, with 15,000,000 passenger miles flown as compared with 8,826,700 in 1961. Our Greenland operation was down slightly, however the AT&T cable patrol was increased to three to four flights per week, with an established route pattern over the international underwater cable routes over the continental shelf east of Trinity Bay.

The purpose of these patrols was to discourage international fishing activities over the cables which were prone to breakage from the dragging of fish nets. The aircraft dropped leaflets printed in five languages advising the foreign fishing trawlers to keep clear. Photographs identifying ships were also taken and sent to AT&T offices in Sydney. Our winter revenue backbone, the winter mail service, was gradually diminishing with the construction of roads making it cheaper for the post office to truck the mail rather than fly it. The Ministry of Transport contract for ice reconnaissance in the Gulf of St. Lawrence came to an end in June when we lost the work to Spartan Air Services.

The bushline operation continued to be utilized, with steady growth in additional contracts of five to six months for Beaver aircraft to Lundrigan Construction, Mines and Technical Surveys, Pichands Mather as well as continued contracts with Mines and Resources, Department of Health and the USAF.

The high cost of operation of Deer Lake airport was becoming a burden, and our efforts to encourage the MOT in assuming this cost continued. In the meantime our Airport Manager Frank LeDrew and his staff were doing yeoman services in keeping the facilities operable under trying conditions. During the year the decision was made to purchase two Handley Page Dart Herald aircraft to update our fleet, and down payments were made accordingly for delivery early 1963.

A study of our organization — with recommendations — was made by Unica Research under K.A. Miller.

As a result of this study, Mr. B.G. Jones was hired as Vice-president of Maintenance and Engineering. Captain Brian Clacken was hired as Chief Pilot, Mainline Operations. I was appointed Vice-president Flight Operations and a Director of the Company, and Roy Cooper was appointed Chief Pilot Bushline operations. As a result of this study, plus the increase in activities, our payroll increased from 123 to 194 employees.

Accidents:

- On March 19 Sikorsky S-55 CF-GHV piloted by Stuart Pollock crashed near Bauline enroute to Bell Island with a load of mail. The landing due to weather was made on unsuitable ground, causing the helicopter to turn over with extensive damage but no injuries to the pilot.
- On May 12 Canso CF-IHA piloted by Captain Vince Keyes crashed on a water landing at Godthab Greenland killing fifteen passengers. The three crew and three passengers managed to escape. The accident was caused by the partial opening of the nose wheel doors,[1] together with glassy water conditions.

Flight Operations 1962

During the year the Government of Newfoundland purchased two Cansos — CF-NWY and CF-IQJ — and had them converted to water-bombers by Field Aviation in Toronto. The aircraft were then turned over to EPA for operation. Those aircraft as modified were to prove a very useful tool in containing forest fires. The eventual addition of five more machines over the years gave the Forestry Service a very impressive and effective fleet.

Three other Cansos — CF-IHN, CF-OFJ and CF-NJC — were also purchased by the company to fulfil commitments in Greenland as well as for general charters and ice and sea patrols.

New pilots joining us in 1962 were Stu Pollack, Ron Penney, Les McInnis, Lionel Clarke, Wolf Poepperl and Stan Tucker.

---

1 The Danish CAA revealed after investigation that the partial opening of the nose wheel doors had been caused by a faulty sequence valve in the hydraulic line to the locking pins, allowing premature activation of the pins, preventing the nose wheel doors from fully closing.

Chapter 18

We Lose Our President

The death of C.A. "Ches" Crosbie on December 26, 1962 was a very severe blow to us all. He had played a very active and effective role in our operation from its inception in 1949. It was his foresight, planning and high inspiration in serving Newfoundland that brought the company to the position it had attained at the time of his death.

I personally had had the opportunity of spending many hours in his company, both in flying him around and in periods of relaxation, and had come to admire his forthrightness and honesty. While he could be very rough if crossed he nevertheless came through as a highly respected businessman and individual.

He always showed a keen interest in the operational side of the company and could be depended upon to take an active hand if necessary. I remember one day in July of 1953. I was in Gander and received a phone call from Ches in St. John's advising me that Pilot Ken Dempster had run the Cessna 180 up on the shoreline at Quidi Vidi Lake after landing, and that he (Ches) had arranged to have it pushed back into the water. He said he had inspected the aircraft floats and that they were ok. He had interrogated the pilot and was satisfied that he was safe to fly so he'd sent him on his way to Gander to report to me on arrival.

It was not unusual for him to appear at the airport at an early hour to wish a "good flight" to me or any of the pilots if they were about to carry out a "First Flight."

His interest and faith kept our little airline together through many lean financial periods. I think it was really due to the respect other companies and businessmen had for him that EPA was permitted to operate for long periods on very thin credit and even a moratorium in the early fifties.

We had all lost a very real friend, and a great business leader.

Chapter 19

Purchase of Handley Page Dart Heralds

With the passing of Chesley A. Crosbie, Mr. Edgar Hickman was approved by the board as Interim Chairman with the appointment of Chesley's son Andrew a few months later. Andrew took up where is father had left off in negotiation with Carl Burke of MCA for the purchase of that company, which was completed on August 30, 1963. As a result of this merger, and to avoid heavy taxation, a new company subsidiary to Maritime Central Airways, now owned by Eastern Provincial Airways, was formed and named Eastern Provincial Airways (1963) Ltd. All assets from the two parent companies were sold and title transferred to the new company. The complete merger was in full operation by October 1, 1963.

With the purchase of MCA and the two Handley Page Dart Heralds it was necessary to obtain a loan of $6,000,000 from the Royal Bank, guaranteed by the Government of Newfoundland. This loan was to be repaid in August 1964 by the issuing of bonds to that total amount.

In late January Captain Clacken, Captain Drover and I went to England, and during the month of February attended ground school and received flight training on the Herald aircraft by Handley Page at Radlett.

We departed March 1 with the first aircraft, CF-EPI, routing via Gatwick, Prestwick, Keflavik, Sondrestrom, Fro-

Handley Page Dart Herald

Hawker Siddley 748

Purchase of Handley Page Dart Heralds 143

British Air Traders Carvair

Boeing 737

bisher, Goose Bay and into Gander. Our second Herald, CF-EPC, was delivered by Captains Rivard and Cooper a month later.

A very intensive training program got underway in the checking out of our crews in order to get the Heralds into operation. This was accomplished by early April with the aircraft being well received by the public.

To facilitate the training program Captain Rivard, on his own initiative, built a Herald Cockpit Procedures Trainer which reduced the number of hours required in the actual aircraft, which substantially reduced the overall cost of training.

With the transfer of MCA licences to EPA (1963) Ltd. the company now had routes covering all the Atlantic Provinces and Labrador. Application was made for the additional points of Sydney and Halifax so it would be possible to join our Newfoundland points with that of the Maritimes.

With the purchase of MCA our fleet received: Two Heralds, CF-NAF and CF-NAC; one DC-4, CF-MCI and three DC-3s, CF-HGL, CF-GOC, CF-FAJ.

EPA (1963) Ltd. now had a fleet of: Four Heralds, six Cansos, two Piper Cubs, two C-46s, two S-55 helicopters, four DC-3s, four Otters, one DC-4, four Cessna 185s and seven Beavers.

In other operations the winter mail service remained good in spite of the increasing road service to the Baie Verte and St. Anthony area. The Greenland operation transported over 9000 passengers between Sondrestrom and the south west points. A Canso was used on the winter service of 63/64 for the first time with the Otter service confined to the Northern points. The cable patrols for AT&T flew over 600 hours of patrol over the eastern continental shelf using a DC-3 equipped with Decca, Loran C, and Radar. This operation was becoming very effective with the customer reporting a decrease in damaged cables as a result of its policing action.

The government activities of wildlife and fire suppression continued, however the water bombers had a relatively light season. Health services remained at a normal level with Otter CF-MIT at St. Anthony and Beaver CF-JAT at North West River. We did however lose the USAF contract at St. Anthony.

Hanger 22 in Gander was purchased from Crown Assets and refitted with a new bonded roof, and with new maintenance workshops constructed.

Late in the year our two C-46s, CF-NAD and CF-NAE, were sold as well as Beavers CF-EYW and CF-IVA.

Financially 1963 — due to the cost of merger with MCA and unexpected associated cost — ended with a loss of $229,000.

Captain Brian Clacken left the company at the end of 1963. During the year as Chief Pilot with EPA he contributed substantially to the training of all line crews on our turbine aircraft. Captain Benoit Rivard succeeded him in that position.

There were several minor accidents involving damage to aircraft. There was one serious accident in which Otter CF-LEA struck a soft spot in the runway while taking-off from the St. Anthony airport and nosed over on its back. There were no injuries to crew or passengers. Another incident involved a Herald which was left without setting the parking brake. It rolled forward hitting the tow tractor and damaged the nose.

With the additional operation and personnel and route system of Maritime Central Airways it was necessary to set the Moncton operation up as a regional operational centre. The operation was managed by Ted Watson as Superintendent of Operations and Captain Garnett Godfrey as Regional Chief Pilot assisted by Captain Bob Mills. Maintenance was managed by Tommy Clarke. Some personnel were transferred to Gander.

This situation continued for several years until the Boeing 737 operation, when a number of crews were transferred from Gander and Moncton to Montreal, and eventually, in 1976, all were consolidated and based at Halifax.

Flight personnel ex-MCA were:

Captains— Garnett Godfrey, Bob Mills, Charlie Trainor, Frank Mitton, Lloyd Gibson, Ray Murneghan, Alex Ballantyne, Bert Ford, Gail Gallagher, John Steeves and Bob Graham.

First Officers— Ross Clements, Elmer Bulman, John Woodley, Lester Ashcroft, Darryl Tanton and Ivan Delong.

Chapter 20

1964 — Eastern Provincial Airways (1963) Ltd.

This was the first complete year of operations of the merged companies of EPA and MCA and, due to the many problems associated with the merger, the financial picture was not good. Passengers carried on schedule operations totalled 95,490, with scheduled aircraft miles flown of 1,141,022. The winter mail service carried 350,000 lbs — down from the previous year of 492,000 lbs due to opening of roads. The bush and Greenland operations maintained the previous year's level

Our total revenues of $5,754,748 against expenses of $6,295,288 resulted in a loss of $540,540.

In our schedule operations we were finally able to connect Newfoundland with the mainland, after the approval and addition of Sydney and Halifax to the Maritime route. Our northern route to Goose and Wabush was still waiting for the development of Churchill Falls and was suffering accordingly.

In our bush operation the Greenland contract with the Danish Government, which would end in June 1965, was going well, with additional income through the full winter. There were associated operating problems caused by operating on water during very low air and water temperatures. These were overcome by our maintenance people modifying the wheel brakes and windshield deicing system, and operating with reduced aircraft loads in accordance with a Wind/Temperature Load graph which we developed.

Government operations increased due to very active water bomber operations in Labrador. Charter and contract operations continued at a normal pace.

In other activities: Deer Lake airport was finally paved and a new passenger terminal built updating our operations there. However we were still pressuring the Department of Transport to take over the airport maintenance, as it was becoming a real financial burden. An ex-MCA DC-3 CF-HGL was sold to Albert Briand of Air St. Pierre, with EPA continuing to operate and maintain it. Another ex-MCA DC-3 — CF-GOC — was written-off in a landing accident at Blanc Sablon on November 21 with no injuries to crew or passengers.

Chapter 21

Conclusion

The purpose of this book has been two-fold. First to attempt to highlight the early activities, operating problems, the financial hardships and successes of Eastern Provincial Airways and, second, to tie in with EPA my own relationships and the memories I have of some of the thousands of flights in various aircraft over the years.

I have chosen to end this book at this point as I feel personally the history of EPA during the first fifteen years to be significantly different from that of the remaining twenty years. I feel its operation was certainly more colourful and pioneering than the latter period, and when I review my own activities over my thirty years with EPA it is for the first fifteen years I experience the most nostalgia. This is not to demean or lessen the importance of the next twenty years as some very significant changes and growth took place. The company developed into a very successful regional air carrier when it divested itself of all its bush activities and concentrated on building its fleet of prop jets and jet aircraft.

The sale of EPA to CP AIR in 1984 saw the closing of a very important chapter of flight history of Eastern Canada, and particularly the Maritimes and Newfoundland Labrador.

Perhaps a book covering the remaining years will follow.

IN MEMORIAM

EPA flight accidents involving fatalities.

May 6, 1956
Helicopter — Bell 47-J (CF-IVF)
    Killed: pilot Gilbert Wass
                 Mrs. Florence Smallwood.
    Survived: Mr. Randy Smallwood
                   Mrs. Richard Morrow
Circumstances: Hit a power line and crashed in flames at Roaches Line, NFLD.

August 29, 1961
DeHavilland DHC-3 Otter (CF-MEX)
    Killed: pilot James Roe
    Survived: crewman Harris Robinson + 4 passengers
Circumstances: Engine fire and forced landing on lake 3 miles north of Sondrestrom, Greenland.

May 12, 1962 Canso PBY-5A CF-IHA
    Killed: 15 passengers
    Survived: Capt. Vince Keyes
                 F/O. Bent Nielsen
                 Flight engineer Mike Woolridge + 3 passengers
Circumstances: aircraft crashed during water landing at Godhaab, Greenland

Mar 17,1965 Herald CF-NAF
    Killed: Capt. Ray Murnaghan
                 F/O. Ross Clements
                 Flight Attendant Doris Chevarie
                 + 5 passengers
Circumstances: aircraft had explosive decompression and crashed 30 miles east of Halifax airport , N.S.

June 23, 1965 Canso Water Bomber CF-OFJ
    Killed: Capt. Paul Bjerg
    Survived: F/O. Max Wiseman
Circumstances: crashed during water pickup at Little Catalina, NFLD

July, 6 1967 Found FBA-2C CF-SVB
    Killed: pilot Neil Bridger + 3 passengers
Circumstances: aircraft stalled and crashed at Williamsport, NFLD

July 12, 1967 Canso Water Bomber CF-NWY
    Killed: Capt. Ronald Penney
               F/O. Yanick Dutin
Circumstances: crashed during water pickup at St. Davids, Bay St. George, NFLD

Jan 1967 Helicopter Sikorsky S-55 CF-HGU
    Killed: pilot Edward Pennell
Circumstances: forced landing after engine failure at St. George, NFLD.

THE EARLY YEARS: PILOTS 1949 TO 1965

1949 — Eric Blackwood; Marsh Jones; Don Patey; Noble Baird (temporary).
1950 — Jack Barton; Hank Hicks; Geo Hudson.
1951 — Jack Bowdery; Ed Lawson; Fred Knox; Carl Fisher.
1952 — Bill Eaton; Gordon MacPherson; Jack Anderson; Kasper Staufacher; Doug Moore; Gerry English; Gerry McGrory.
1953 — Dave Luke; Ivan Demoine; Ben Rivard, (chief pilot sched ops 1964 – 68); Bev Croft; Ken Dempster; Julian Moraze; Chris Madsen; Jack Kielley; A.J. Lewington.
1954 — Roy Cooper; Rex Clibbery; Gunner Laurell; Stewart Legassick; Bob Packer.
1955 — Don Ballantyne; Glen McCluskey; Cyril Jones; Al Roach.
1956 — Jim Roe; Clayton Hutchings; Geoff Henderson; Peter Crux; Ian Massie; Gill Wass.
1957 — Austin Garrett; Ron Anonsen; Ron Smith; LLoyd Batten; Robin LeDrew.
1958 — Harry Drover; Hubert Rodway; Ray Taylor; Andre Charron.
1960 — Paul Bjerg; Eric Brorup; Len Byl; Walter Brown.
1961 — Ellie Yeomans; Dave McNeil; Cliff Fielding; Dave Lang; Bent Nielsen; Boyd Hefford; Maurice Charron; Syd Greeley; Vince Keyes; Pete Chalmers.
1962 — Stuart Pollock; Ron Penney; Les McInnis; Lionel Clarke; Wolf Poepperl; Stan Tucker.
1963 — Brian Clacken; Hal Lowe; Jim Sterling; Tom Green; George Pinkney; Capt Garnett Godfrey, ex-MCA Regional chief pilot.
1963 – 1976 — Bob Mills ex-MCA, Assistant chief pilot.
1963 — Charlie Trainor, ex-MCA; Pappy Mitton, ex-MCA; Doug Stults, ex-MCA; Lloyd Gibson, ex-MCA; Ray Murnahan, ex-MCA; Alex Ballantyne, ex-MCA; Bert Ford,

chief pilot 1968-1973; Gail Gallagher, ex-MCA; John Steeves, ex-MCA; Bob Graham, ex-MCA; F/O Ivan Delong, ex-MCA; Darryl Tanton, ex-MCA; Elmer Bulman, ex-MCA; John Woodley, ex-MCA; Ross Clements, ex-MCA; Lester Ashcroft, ex-MCA.

1965 — John Ivanoskoff; Stirling Lush; Gustaffson; Bob Warren; Dave Robertson; John Grace; Ches Walker.

THE EARLY YEARS 1949 – 1963
Maintenance people I remember

Engineers — Bill Harris; Jim Duke; Jack Phennel; John Collins; Art Wildish; Glen Hefford; Bob Walsh; Bob Briggs; Ches Sparks, Walter Rockwood (radio); George Furey, Joe Lear(radio); Mike Trainor, Fred Smeaton (motor mechanic); Gerry Finn, Benny Doyle (stores); Clayton Hodge, Bob Carter (stores); Cyril Ivimey, Tom Godden (stores); Morris Power, Norm Sheppard. Engineer; Harry Seaward, John Peyton Engineer; Tommy Clark ex-MCA; Lofty McGinn ex-MCA; Kevin White; Bill Clifford; Doug Jewer; Mike Woolridge, flight engineer/engineer; Frank Ireland; Len Parsons; Roland Philpot; George Petrie.

FLIGHT DISPATCH – OPERATIONS CENTER

Jimmy Clark; Jim Davis; Bert Patey; Cliff Seymour, o.i.c. ops center 1960 – 1978; Rod Goff; George Fowlow; Harvey Rideout; Don James; Jack Furey — Dispatch and flight engineer on Canso aircraft; Lloyd Brown; Johnny Brown, ex-MCA; Stuart Girvan, ex-MCA; Reg White, ex-MCA; E.P. Ted Watson, ex-MCA, Regional Supt operations (Moncton); Maurice Doyle; Nathan Dyke; Des Griffin; Walter Mesh; Pop Cudmore, ex-MCA.

THE EARLY YEARS — ADMINISTRATION and OFFICE

Elizabeth Holland, office manager 1949 – 1954
Mel Davis, office assistant 1953 – 19 ?
John Anstey, office manager 1953 – 1956
Barb Nugent, secretary 1954 – 1956
Jim Macgillavry, office manager 1956 - 1959
Maggie Cashin, secretary 1956 –
Frank Newhook, office manager 1956 –
Gerry Mahoney, traffic manager 1960 – 1963
Harvey Kelly, traffic manager 1963 – 1965, Personnel manager 1965 –
Gaston Winter, Accountant.

THE EARLY YEARS 1949 – 1964
Financial:

1949 – 1952 unknown as record were lost in a fire at Crosbie & Co

Revenues Expenses Income:

Year	Revenues	Expenses	Income
1953	$ 356,382.00	$ 378,996.00	$ (736.00)
1954	404,745.00	390,824.00	3921.00
1955	555,459.00	519,398.00	36,061.00
1956	1,191,195.00	1,175,269.00	15,926.00
1957	896,174.00	820,536.00	75,638.00
1958	Not available		
1959	1,139,320.00	1,110,936.00	28,384.00
1960	1,615,214.00	1,537,158.00	78,056.00
1961	2,181,414.00	2,109,611.00	71,803.00
1962	2,518,408.00	2,542,787.00	(24,379.00)
1963	Merge with Maritime Central Airways		(229,000.00)
1964	5,754,748.00	6,295,288.00	(540,540.00)

THE EARLY YEARS 1949 – 1964.

Management:

Eric Blackwood, General Manager & Founder 1949 – 1951

Marsh Jones, Chief Pilot 1951 – 1956, Operations Manager 1956 – 1959, Director Flight Operations 1959 - 1962, Vice President Flight Ops 1959 – 1962

Bill Harris, Operations Manager 1951 – 1954, Assistant Manager 1954 – 1962, Vice President Traffic & Sales 1962 – 1972, Vice President Industry & Government Affairs 1972

Farrel Gaudet, Director Industrial Relations 1963 - 1970, Vice-President Traffic & Sales 1970 - 1981

Brian Jones, Vice President Maintenance 1963 – 1984

Harold Wareham, Secretary Treasurer 1964 – 1970, Vice-President Finance 1970 - 1980

Jim Lewington, General Manager 1954 – 1959, President & Director 1959 – 1980

Board of Directors:

Chesley A. Crosbie, President 1949 – 1959, Chairman 1959 - 1962

Directors — Charles R. Bell, 1949 – 1963; Edgar L. Hickman, 1949 – 1963; Bernard Parsons 1949 – 1963; Frank O'Leary, 1949 – 1953; Jim Lewington, 1959 – 1984; Bill Harris, 1962 – 1978; Marsh Jones, 1962 – 1979; Andrew Crosbie, 1962 – 1978; Keith Miller, 1962 – 1984.

AIRCRAFT FLEET 1965

Handley Page Herald, 3; Douglas DC-4, 1; Douglas DC-3, 4; PBY 5A Canso, 2; Canso Water Bombers, 4; DHC–3 Otters, 5; DHC–2 Beavers, 5; S-55 helicopters, 3; Piper PA 18, 2.

AIRCRAFT TYPES OPERATED BY EPA

Piper Cubs PA12 and PA 18 Super Cub
Cessna Crane T50
Norseman Mk IV and VI
De Havilland Beaver DHC-2 and Turbo Beaver
De Havilland Otter DHC-3
De Havilland Twin-Otter DHC-6
Republic Seebee RC-3
Stinson Station Wagon 108-3
Avro Anson Mk V
Cessna 170
Cessna 180
Cessna 185
Bell 47J
Piaggio Royal Gull
Lockheed 10
Douglas DC-3
Consolidated Canso PBY-5A
Curtis C-46
Sikorsky S55
Handley Page Dart Herald
Douglas DC-4 and Douglas Carvair
Beech Baron B-55
Found FBA2C
Hawker Siddley 748
Boeing 737